First World War
and Army of Occupation
War Diary
France, Belgium and Germany

42 DIVISION
Divisional Troops
211 Brigade Royal Field Artillery
1 March 1917 - 24 March 1919

WO95/2649/2

The Naval & Military Press Ltd
www.nmarchive.com
Published in association with The National Archives

Published by

The Naval & Military Press Ltd

Unit 10 Ridgewood Industrial Park,

Uckfield, East Sussex,

TN22 5QE England

Tel: +44 (0) 1825 749494

www.naval-military-press.com

www.nmarchive.com

This diary has been reprinted in facsimile from the original. Any imperfections are inevitably reproduced and the quality may fall short of modern type and cartographic standards.

© **Crown Copyright**
Images reproduced by permission of The National Archives, London, England, 2015.

Contents

Document type	Place/Title	Date From	Date To
Heading	WO95/2649/2		
Heading	211th Brigade R.F.A. Mar 1917 Mar 1919		
Miscellaneous	War Diary Of 24th Field Artillery Brigade From 1st March 1917 To 31st March 1917		
War Diary	Ref Map Abbeville 1,100,000	01/03/1917	24/03/1917
War Diary	Grand Laviers	20/03/1917	28/03/1917
War Diary	Ref Map Abbeville 1,100,000	29/03/1917	31/03/1917
Heading	War Diary Of 211th Brigade R.F.A. From 1.4.17 To 30.4.17		
War Diary	Ref Map. Abbeville 1,100,000	01/04/1917	03/04/1917
War Diary	Ref Map Amiens C.I 1,100,000	03/04/1917	04/04/1917
War Diary	Hamelet (Amiens) B.2	05/04/1917	05/04/1917
War Diary	Bois Olympe (Amiens) J 1.1	06/04/1917	06/04/1917
War Diary	Bois Olympe	07/04/1917	08/04/1917
War Diary	Amiens 1,100,000 Z I	08/04/1917	08/04/1917
War Diary	Ref Map St Quentin 1,100,000	09/04/1917	21/04/1917
War Diary	Villiers Faucon Ref Map 62.c 1.1.40.000	22/04/1917	30/04/1917
Heading	War Diary Of C.Btty. 211th Bde R.F.A. From April 10th 1917 To April 30th 1917.		
War Diary	Epehy France	10/04/1917	30/04/1917
Heading	War Diary Of 211th Brigade R.F.A. From 1-5-17 To 31.5.17 Volume 2		
War Diary		13/05/1917	19/05/1917
War Diary	Gillemont Farm	20/05/1917	22/05/1917
War Diary	Havrincourt Wood	23/05/1917	29/05/1917
War Diary		01/05/1917	13/05/1917
Heading	War Diary Of 211th Brigade RFA. From 1-6-17 To 30-6-17 Volume II		
War Diary	France	02/06/1917	05/06/1917
War Diary	Ref. Map. Ribecourt. 1/20,000. Sheet I	05/06/1917	29/06/1917
Heading	War Diary Of 211th Brigade RFA. From July 1st To July 31st 1917 Volume II		
War Diary	Reference Map, 57c. N.E. 1,20,000	01/07/1917	31/07/1917
Heading	War Diary. Of 211th Brigade RFA From Aug 1/17 To Aug 31/17		
War Diary		01/08/1917	31/08/1917
Heading	War Diary Of 211th Bde R.F.A. From 1-9-17 To 30-9-17 Vol VII		
War Diary		04/09/1917	30/09/1917
Heading	War Diary Of 211th Brigade RFA From October 1st To October 31st Vol VIII		
War Diary	In The Field	01/10/1917	30/10/1917
Heading	War Diary Of 211th Bde R.F.A. From 1-11-17 To 30-11-17 Vol VIII		
War Diary	Course	01/11/1917	01/11/1917
War Diary	Posting	02/11/1917	03/11/1917
War Diary	Course	03/11/1917	04/11/1917
War Diary	Appointment Leave Award	05/11/1917	05/11/1917
War Diary	Course	08/11/1917	08/11/1917
War Diary	Leave Strength	14/11/1917	14/11/1917

War Diary	Awards	16/11/1917	17/11/1917
War Diary	Movement	19/11/1917	23/11/1917
War Diary	Course	23/11/1917	23/11/1917
War Diary	Transfer Leave		
War Diary	Movement	24/11/1917	24/11/1917
War Diary	Movement	25/11/1917	26/11/1917
War Diary	Awards	28/11/1917	28/11/1917
War Diary	Movement	30/11/1917	30/11/1917
Heading	War Diary of 211th Brigade R.F.A. From 1st December 1917 to 31st December 1917 Volume II		
War Diary		01/12/1917	31/12/1917
Heading	War Diary of 211th Brigade R.F.A. From 1st January 1918 to 31st January 1918 Volume III		
War Diary		01/01/1918	31/01/1918
Heading	War Diary Of 211th Brigade R.F.A. From 1st. February 1918 to 28th. February 1918 Volume III		
War Diary	In The Field	01/02/1918	28/02/1918
Heading	211th Brigade Royal Field Artillery March 1918		
Miscellaneous	211 Bde RFA War Diary March 1918 From 1/3/18 to 31/3/18 Volume 15		
War Diary		03/03/1918	31/03/1918
Heading	211th Brigade, R.F.A. April 1918		
Miscellaneous	War Diary Of 211th Brigade R.F.A. From 1st. April 1918 to 30th April 1918 Volume 16		
War Diary	In the Field	01/02/1918	30/04/1918
Heading	War Diary Of 211th Brigade R.F.A. From 1st. May 1918 to 31st. May 1918 Volume 17		
War Diary	Field	02/05/1918	29/05/1918
Heading	War Diary Of 211th Brigade R.F.A. From 1st June 1918 to 30th June 1918 Volume 18		
War Diary	Field	01/06/1918	26/06/1918
Heading	War Diary Of 211th Brigade R.F.A. From 1st July 1918 to 31st July 1918 Volume 19		
War Diary	Field	01/07/1918	31/07/1918
Heading	War Diary Of 211th Brigade R.F.A. From 1st August 1918 to 31st August 1918 Volume 20		
War Diary	Field	02/08/1918	31/08/1918
Heading	211th Brigade R.F.A. War Diary September 1918 Volume No 20		
War Diary	In The Field	01/09/1918	30/09/1918
Heading	211th Brigade R.F.A. War Diary October 1918 Volume No 21		
War Diary	Field	01/10/1918	31/10/1918
Heading	211th Brigade R.F.A. War Diary November 1918 Volume No 22		
War Diary	In The Field	01/11/1918	26/11/1918
Heading	211th Brigade R.F.A. War Diary December 1918 Volume No 23		
War Diary	In The Field	01/12/1918	29/12/1918
Heading	211th Brigade R.F.A. War Diary January 1919 Volume No 24		
War Diary	Montignies Sur-sambre	01/01/1919	26/01/1919
Heading	War Diary 211th Brigade R.F.A. February 1919 Volume No 25		
War Diary	Montignies Sur Sambre	02/02/1919	27/02/1919

Heading	War Diary 211th Brigade R.F.A. March 19 Volume No 26		
War Diary	Montignies Sur Sambre	01/03/1919	24/03/1919

WO 95
2649/2

42ND DIVISION

211TH BRIGADE R.F.A.
MAR ~~FEB~~ 1917-MAR 1919

Vol 2

Confidential

War Diary

of

2nd Field Artillery Brigade

From 1st March 1917 To 31st March 1917

(Volume 3. 1917.)

Army Form C. 2118.

WAR DIARY

INTELLIGENCE SUMMARY

(Erase heading not required.)

Instructions regarding War Diaries and Intelligence Summaries are contained in F.S. Regs., Part II. and the Staff Manual respectively. Title Pages will be prepared in manuscript.

Place	Date	Hour	Summary of Events and Information	Remarks and references to Appendices
REF MAP	1/3/17	1730	Brigade Enroute to MARSEILLES. Transport left MALTA at (Feb 28th)	CRW
ABBEVILLE	2/3/17		Enroute MARSEILLES	CRW
1.100.000	3/3/17		" " "	CRW
	4/3/17		Arrived MARSEILLES 0800. Entrained "C" Battery train departed 2000.	CRW
	5/3/17		Entrained "A" Battery with portion of H.Qrs. Train departed 0830.	CRW
			" "B" " " " " " " 1235.	CRW
	6/3/17		Enroute NORTH of FRANCE.	CRW
	7/3/17		All units detrained PONT REMY. marched through ABBEVILLE to Billets at GRAND LAVIERS.	CRW
	8/3/17		Cleaning billets which were in a filthy condition.	CRW
	9/3/17		Training Remounts taken over at Alexandria	CRW
	10/3/17		No entry. LIEUT L.S. DALE to Hospital.	CRW
	11/3/17		Church Parade. LIEUT. L.D. MACK rejoined from leave in U.K. 10/3/17	CRW
	12/3/17		Battery Training.	CRW
	13/3/17		Inspection by Major Genl B.R. MITFORD. C.B. D.S.O. G.O.C. 42nd Division. These Officers were in Billets at PETIT LAVIERS	CRW
			LIEUT MACKENZIE Y 32 OR BAC. reported arrival	CRW
	14/3/17		D/211 arrived PONT REMY & proceeded to Billets at PORT-LE-GRAND	CRW
	15/3/17		Battery Training Proceeding.	CRW

WAR DIARY
or
INTELLIGENCE SUMMARY

Army Form C. 2118.

Place	Date	Hour	Summary of Events and Information	Remarks and references to Appendices
1st MAR ABBEVILLE 1.100.000	16/3/17 17/3/17		Battery Training proceeding. The advance party from 211th Bde which left EGYPT FEB 3rd returned from attachment with 1st DIVISION R.A. near DOMPIERRE (See entry Feb 1st)	Ch— Ch—
	18/3/17		2/LIEUT HALLET'S attachment ceased and he reported to O.C. 210th. 18-18 PR ORDNANCE drawn at ABBEVILLE. Brigade for duty.	Ch—
	19/3/17		The following received Certificates from Signalling School ZEITOUN 2/Lieut ALMOND — 20 words per min. 18" Hewith.J.M.— G.T. Grierson J. — Dr Whittle.S.— Dr Whalley J.T. 1st class signallers.	Ch—
	20/3/17		Battery Training proceeding	Ch—
	21/3/17		— ditto —	Ch—
	22/3/17		— ditto —	Ch—
	23/3/17		Brigade Route March F.S.M.O. The Brigade was inspected "Enroute" by the B.G.R.A. who expressed his satisfaction with the "Turn out"	Ch—
	24/3/17		POSTINGS 2/LIEUT L. BUCK from D/211 Bde to No 2 Sec 42" D.A.C. — " C.I. SEACROFT " No 2 Sec 42" D.A.C. replaced him. SUMMER TIME was adopted, all clocks being advanced one hour at 11.pm. 2/Lieut A.C. SANDYS to hospital	Ch—

WAR DIARY
or
INTELLIGENCE SUMMARY
(Erase heading not required.)

Army Form C. 2118.

Place	Date	Hour	Summary of Events and Information	Remarks and references to Appendices
GRAND LAVIERS	25/3/17		No Entry	
	26/3/17		LIEUT W.N. HOUGH proceeded to England on Leave 10 days from 29th departure. D/211-2 OTR - B/211-2OR C/211-1OR D/211-1OR	Ceo
	27/3/17		LIEUT R.M. GARNETT - LIEUT KEARNS - LIEUT KNOWLES - LIEUT MARKS proceeded to School of Gunnery VAUX for course of instruction. R.S.M. BOWKER B/211 Battery proceeded to England in 10 days leave Conference at a meeting of OC Batteries it was decided that it would be advisable to run separate canteens at the front for each Battery rather than have a Brigade canteen as units might possibly be far apart. Also that the sum of £50 the Final Allotment to the Brigade from the HELLES Canteen Fund should be divided among Batteries. See copies of the Establishment. Signals The 12 hour system of timing messages was again taken into use namely AM-PM. LIEUT GAS COLLEN took over the duties of adjutant during the temp. absence of Lt. & PM GARNETT. The Brigade sounded in F.S.M.O at 1AM. and proceeded by Route March thro GRAND LAVIERS - BUIGNY - ST MACLOU - ST NICHOLAS - ABBEVILLE	Ceo
	28/3/17		Hospital admissions - Major C.A. VALENTINE D/211 admitted Hosp! 27/3/17 Capt L. HIGHTON from B.A.C. assumes Command of D/211 during the absence of Major Valentine.	Ceo

2449 Wt. W14957/M90 750,000 1/16 J.B.C. & A. Forms/C.2118/12.

WAR DIARY or INTELLIGENCE SUMMARY

Army Form C. 2118.

Place	Date	Hour	Summary of Events and Information	Remarks and references to Appendices
GRAND LAVIERS	28/3/17		Hospital, admission to – Capt C.R. Brown A/211 to troops	Chus
Ref. MAP ABBEVILLE 1:100,000	29/3/17		Battery training proceeding	Chus
	30/3/17		— " — — " — — " —	Chus
	31/3/17		— " — — " — — " —	Chus

Vol 3

Confidential

War Diary
of
211th Brigade R.F.A.

From 1.4.17 to 30.4.17

(Volume 4. 1917)

Chancter Lieut. Col.
Comdg. 211th F.A. Bde.

WAR DIARY or INTELLIGENCE SUMMARY

Army Form C. 2118.

Place	Date	Hour	Summary of Events and Information	Remarks and references to Appendices
REF MAP 1.4.17				
ABBEVILLE 1:100,000			The undermentioned officers & men rejoined their unit from a course of instruction at VAUX nr AMIENS. LIEUT G.W.H. ARKS B/211. LIEUT F KNOWLES B/211. LIEUT H.W.L. KEARTS	Chw
			A/211 LIEUT R.M. GARNETT. ADJUTANT. 1093 Sgt. CHARNLEY B/211. 1153 A Bt. ABBOTT. A/211. 1585 Corpl. LOGAN C/211. 919 Bt. ZELLAR D/211. 2 LIEUT G.H. DREWRY to Hospital.	Chw
- " -	3/4/17		Draft of Officers - Rein'd GIBBS. H.B.S. att. A/211	Chw
			- " - WALKER E.C. B/211	
			- " - LOWTHER G C/211	Chw
R/MAP AMIENS 1:100,000 C.I	4/4/17		Move to SAINT SAUVEUR Brigade moved from ABBEVILLE area and billeted for night 4/5th at ST SAUVEUR 21 miles. Started 8AM arrived 6pm.	Chw
HAMELET (AMIENS) G.2	5/4/17		Brigade moved on to HAMELET leaving ST SAUVEUR at 9 am arrived 4pm. Distance 12 miles were in billets	Chw
BOIS OLYMPE (AMIENS) [J.1.]	6/4/17		Brigade moved to BOIS OLYMPE and were in billets v dug outs. The horse lines were quite unsuitable the horses etc the approaches to them being deep liquid mud.	

Army Form C. 2118.

Instructions regarding War Diaries and Intelligence Summaries are contained in F.S. Regs., Part II. and the Staff Manual respectively. Title Pages will be prepared in manuscript.

WAR DIARY
INTELLIGENCE SUMMARY

(Erase heading not required.)

Place	Date	Hour	Summary of Events and Information	Remarks and references to Appendices
BOIS OLYMPE	7/4/17		Draft of Officers. The following officers reported for duty and were attached to units as under:— Lieut A.B. DYKE A/211 — Lieut R.M.C. McIVER B/211 — " F.A. MOOLENAAR C/211 — " C.T. POTHECARY D/211	CRW
	8/4/17		Advance Party to 48th Division. Lieut. Col. C.E. Walker, Major J. Nall, Capt. L. Heighton and Adjutant Lieut R.M. Ganch went forward. In attachment to 46th Div. arty. & were joined by Capt R.N. Bernyield and Capt Stott (who were already forward) the whole acting as a Reconnoitring Party for the Brigade.	CRW
AMIENS 1,100,000 21	-"-		Move to DOINGT (1/40,000 62 C.) The 211th Brigade with 161 Sec BAC moved to DOINGT and bivouaced in an open field under the Command of Major D Brown	CRW
" Ry MAP ST QUENTIN 1.100,000	9/4/17		Move to VILLIERS FAUCON (1/40,000 62 C.) The Brigade moved on to VILLIERS FAUCON and A/211 B/211 came under orders of Col LORD HYFORD OC 240 B32 C/211 & D/211 came under orders of Col COLVILLE OC 241 B32 Wagon Lines were formed at TEMPLEUX LA FOSSE	BW
	11/4/17		Compliments: The following complimentary message was received from Brig Genl F.W.H. WALSHE. D.S.O Comdg. 42 Div Arty (1) On results of Course at VAUX School of Gunnery. The Officers were particularly keen & will up to their work, their knowledge of Gunnery and the practical employment of Field Arty being considerably above the average Standard of Officers who attend Courses here. The cable officer	CRW

Sch 249. Wt.W14957/M99-759,09 1/16 J.B.C. & A Forms/C.2118/12. to the N.C.O's who worked well.

Army Form C. 2118.

WAR DIARY
INTELLIGENCE SUMMARY
(Erase heading not required.)

Place	Date	Hour	Summary of Events and Information	Remarks and references to Appendices
	11/4/17		(Compliments Contd) (2) On March discipline of Brigade — "The C.R.A. has been much gratified with the great improvement in march discipline exhibited during the forward move. Both the Divisional Commander and M.G. R.A. 4th Army saw the march to-day and they both pronounced the discipline to be excellent"	Chr
	12/4/17		Gas instruction for Brigade carried out so far as possible at BOIS OLYMPE on 8" mist.) N°1120 G.m.u.185 Dy211 wounded (Slight)	Cru
	13/4/17		The following officers are posted to Brigade artly R.P.Orelle- H.2 Div. 2Lt G.113BS H.10.S. 9/2" 2Lt DYKE A.B. A/211. 2Lt WALKE 13/211 2Lt McIVER 15/211 — 2Lt LOWTHER G. C/211. 2Lt MOOLENAAR C/211 2Lt POTHECARY Dy211.	Chr
	14/4/17		2Lt W.N. HOUGH returned from leave (U.K.) N°1055 Sgt METCALFE H. A/211 proceeded to Base pending commission	Cru
	15/4/17		2Lt Brewry & 2Lt A.C. Sandys returned from Hospital to duty.	Cru
	17/4/17		Lieut C.A.S. COLLIN D/211 posted to Brigade H.Q.- Lieut W.N. HOUGH H.Q.- D/211	Cru Cru
	18/4/17		Capt S.P. STOTT C/211 proceeds on leave to England (10 days)	Cru
	19/4/17 21/4/17		No Entry —	Cru

Army Form C. 2118.

WAR DIARY
INTELLIGENCE SUMMARY
(Erase heading not required.)

Place	Date	Hour	Summary of Events and Information	Remarks and references to Appendices
VILLIERS FAUCON NEAR MAP 62C 1/40,000	22/4/17		Lieut Col. C.E. WALKER. T.D assumed TACTICAL Command of C/211 & B/2/41 for operations in connection with attack on TROIL & GUILLEMONT FARM and relinquished Command 2nd "inst".	Chd
	21/4/17		Lieut E. HOLDEN 15th HUSSARS & batman att to Bde HQrs	Chd
	22/4/17		Lieut C.E. KESSLER C/211 returned from course of instruction at VAUX. Lieut H.B.S. GIBBS A/211 proceeded on course of instruction to VAUX.	Chd
	23/4/17		28 OR Bde TMB att to units	Chd
	25/4/17		Lieut J ALMOND D/211 returned from leave to England.	Chd
	27/4/17		2292 Gr JOHNSON. C.R B/211 Wounded by Shell on 26/4/17	Chd
	28/4/17		Capt S.R. STOTT C/211 granted extension leave to 8/5/7/17 "URGent Private Affairs" Authy W.O.	Chd
	"		Lieut Al MAKINSON 1/5" MANCHESTER att to Brigade for duty as Signal Officer with Signal Sub Sec R.F.A. 2Lt J ALMOND D/211 att B/211 for duty.	Chd

WAR DIARY
&
INTELLIGENCE SUMMARY

(Erase heading not required.)

Army Form C. 2118.

Place	Date	Hour	Summary of Events and Information	Remarks and references to Appendices
In the Line 29/4/17	29.4.17		Casualties - N° 104129 Gr. LOCHRENE. P.G. T.M.B att C/211 wounded in arm (Shrapnel) 28/4/17 N° 107542. Gr. MIELL.H. T.M.B. att C/211 wounded in neck (Shrapnel) 28/4/17	Cas
	30/4/17		Casualties - N° 116204 Gr. NOLAN.D. T.M.B att C/211 wounded (Shrapnel) by 29.4.17 N° 1576 G. HETHERINGTON. W. C/211 wounded (Shrapnel) by 29.4.17	Cas

Cloake, Lieut. Col.
GGNDg. 21t TM T.A Bde

CONFIDENTIAL
WAR DIARY
OF
"C" BTTY. 211TH BDE. R.F.A. (whilst attached to the 241st. Bde. R.F.A.)

FROM APRIL 10th 1917   TO   APRIL 30th 1917.

WAR DIARY
INTELLIGENCE SUMMARY

(Erase heading not required.)

Army Form C. 2118.
Page 1

C" Battery 211th Fld. Brigade. attached 2 Hist. Bde. R.F.A.

Place	Date	Hour	Summary of Events and Information	Remarks and references to Appendices
EPEHY FRANCE	10/4/17	8.15 p.m.	Battery took up a position in action under cover, but not in view, at E.5.c. 81, 53 with an observation post at X.25.a.33 covering a front normally of 15° at 2600, and supporting the Left half battalion of the formation.	SHEET 62° NE 57° SE
"	11/4/17	9.0 a.m.	Carried out registration of BEET FACTORY and S.O.S. lines in front of Battery front in X.25.a.54 to X.25.c.78	T.K.
"	12/4/17		Carried out further registration and fired on BEET FACTORY. (Wireless stn established at E.5.a.4.2.)	T.K.
"	13/4/17		Registered the PEIZIÈRE - GUISLAIN road in X.17.a.72 and X.18.c. one gun on this road fired accurately with a view to driving off an armoured car attack.	T.K.
"	14/4/17		Observation for firing any good. Few rounds fired on BEET FACTORY and roads leading to "	T.K.
"	15/4/17		Observation impossible.	T.K.
"	16/4/17		At 4am, 5am and 5.45am Battery fired 5 rounds per gun at section fire 20 seconds on enemy trenches in X.22.a and X.22.c.	T.K.
"	17/4/17		Registered new S.O.S lines in X.15.d.50 to X.22.c.33, also the line X.21.a.84 to X.22.a.75 and MEUNIER HOUSE X.8.d. and PETIT SAUT RAVINE X.9.c. At 4.25 a.m. the Battery opened fire on the enemys trenches west just EAST of MEUNIER HOUSE then lifted 100 yards at a time on to the road via X.9.c. and lifted again to track PETIT SAUT RAVINE firing in all 600 rounds. This fire was to support the 8th Division on our left to take VILLERS-GUISLAIN.	T.K.
"	18/4/17		F.O.O. established at the cross roads in X.22.c.66. S.O.S. lines were registered in front of Infantry trenches running from PIGEON to TARGELLE RAVINE	T.K. T.K.
	19/4/17 20/4/17 21/4/17		Enemy quiet except at long long range	T.K.

Army Form C. 2118.

Page 2.

"C" Battery 211th F.A. Brigade attached 2111th Bde. R.F.A.

WAR DIARY
or
INTELLIGENCE SUMMARY
(Erase heading not required.)

Place	Date	Hour	Summary of Events and Information	Remarks and references to Appendices
EPEHY FRANCE	22/4/17	3 a.m.	The Battery moves to a new position further forward in F8a 25.25 with an observation post in PETIT PRIEL FARM, F4b.7%.	
	23/4/17		Registration carried out of PRIEL FARM – VENDHUILE ROAD in F6a and the TOMBOIS FARM – VENDHUILE ROAD in F6a.	
	24/4/17		The Battery supported an attack on GILLEMONT FARM A13a and the KNOLL (high ground in F6b) The SOS barrage was not called for, but Phase 2, 500 yards EAST of the trenches in F6a as far as S.25E was fired at 4.50am and 4.50am.	SHEET 62 B N.W.
	25/4/17		at 11.20 a.m. Battery fired on enemy trenches on high ground in F6a and X.30 chasing them out.	
			Battery fired 20 rounds per hour on enemy trenches in X.30a.70 to F6a.95, during hours of daylight, searching to a distance of 400 yards	
			At 9.0 p.m. the SOS went up on the Battery's front and fire opened immediately at 3 rounds a minute for the 1st (No 50?) first 5 minutes then 1 per minute until orders to stop. 500 rounds fired.	
	26/4/17		During the day Battery fired bursts of fire on same enemy trenches.	
			At 9.9 p.m. S.O.S. went up on (battery?) on the right and fire opened on our SOS lines at prescribed rate. S.O.S. firing was ordered 15 minutes later.	
	27/4/17		Battery fired to 40 rounds during daylight and 40 rounds at night to be expended as ordinarial bursts of fire and sweeping shots on enemy trenches and approaches to VENDHUILE	
	28/4/17		Battery limited to 40 rounds by day and 20 by night, methods and duration of fire as yesterday	

Army Form C. 2118.
Page 3.

WAR DIARY
or
INTELLIGENCE SUMMARY
(Erase heading not required.)

"C" Battery 211th FA Bde. attached 2nd Sh Bde R.F.A.

Place	Date	Hour	Summary of Events and Information	Remarks and references to Appendices
EPHHEY	29/4/17		At 6.30 a.m. enemy artillery 15 cm opened fire in the vicinity of Battery Position and kept this up for 3 hours. 6 other ranks were casualties.	
FRANCE	30/4/17		Slight firing for the Battery. 20 rounds on VENDHUILE approaches. Firing finished as yesterday.	

J. Hubert Runger
C Battery 211th FA Bde.

Vol 4

Confidential.

War Diary
of
211th Brigade R.F.A.

From 1-5-17. To 31-5-17.

Volume 2.

WAR DIARY
INTELLIGENCE SUMMARY

Army Form C. 2118.

Place	Date 1917 MAY	Hour	Summary of Events and Information	Remarks and references to Appendices
	13.		COURSES: Artillery School, VAUX. Lieut. M.E. THOMPSON D/211. Proceeded to School. 2/Lt. A.C. Sandys. A/211.	Chn
	14.		ATTACHMENT: Lieut. L.D. MACK, A/211, Attached to Headquarters, 211. LEAVE: Lieut. G.A.S. COLLIN Proceeded on 10 days leave to U.K. (A.V.C. Attached). Captain R.M. AULTON -do- Major D. BROWN.? B/211 -do-	Chn
	15.		27 Other Ranks posted from 42nd D.A.C. to Brigade, distribution, HQ/211, 2, A/211 - 12, B/211 - 9, C/211 - 2, D/211 - 2.	Chn
	17.		Lieut. C.E. KESSLER, C/211 sick to Hospital.	Chn
	18.		AEROPLANE SHOOT A/211: A/211 registered a target in S.19.d.1.5. by means of an Aeroplane.	Chn
	19.		Captain A.C. TRENCH (Chaplain) on leave to U.K., 10 Days.	Chn
GILLEMONT FARM.	20.	3.35 am.	S.O.S. in RIGHT SUB. GROUP: At 3.35 am an S.O.S. Rocket was sent up at GILLEMONT FARM A.20.c.5.0. and the 211th Brigade (Left Sub. Group) was ordered by C.R.A. to support the Bombardment of the Right Sub Group (210th Brigade) A/211 and C/211 were ordered to do this firing at the rate of 1 round per gun per minute, ceasing at 4-30 am on order of C.R.A. D/211 fired with one section on cross ROADS, VENDHUILLE, at the rate of one round per gun per minute. The S.O.S. Rocket was reported by 211th Brigade Lookout Officer as being at a bearing of 118° from his O.P. in EPEHY, F.1.b.1.6. The feature of the show was the excellent way the communications were maintained, no difficulty being found in speaking in any direction. The attack on the Farm was unsuccessful. RELIEF by 296th Brigade R.F.A. During the night of 20/21st One section of each battery was relieved and returned to the Wagon Line, TEMPLEUX. LA FOSSE.	Chn
	21st.		Relief completed. Remainder of Brigade was relieved by 296th Brigade and returned to Wagon Line, TEMPLEUX. Relief completed by 12 Midnight, 21/22nd.	Chn
	22.		VALLULART WOOD: Brigade marched to VALLULART WOOD, P.32.b.8.1., starting 11-30am. and arriving 2-30 pm.; distance of 9 miles. Continued.	Chn

WAR DIARY
or
INTELLIGENCE SUMMARY
(Erase heading not required.)

Army Form C. 2118.

Place	Date	Hour	Summary of Events and Information	Remarks and references to Appendices
HAVRIN-COURT WOOD.	1917 May 23.		During the night of 23/24th one section of each battery moved as follows:— A/211 to Q.20.d.3.5. relieving A/91st, 20th Division. B/211 to Q.13.b.7.3. relieving B/91st, 20th Division. D/211 to Q.8.d.8.6. relieving D/91st, 20th Division.	CRW
			C/211 came under orders of Major Browning who was given command of right GROUP R.A. 42nd Division. —do— Left Section, D/211 —do—	CRW
	24.		Night of 24/25th remainder of Batteries relieved and Brigade Headquarters moved to P.18.c.7.6. and Lieut. Colonel Walker T.D. took over command of Centre Group R.A. 42nd Division Front.	CRW
	25.		During night of 25/26th Right Group Commander called for support to repel a raid and B/211 and D/211 were detailed to assist, firing at a rate of 2 rounds per gun per minute for 18 prs and 1 round per gun per for Howitzers. The call for this support was TEDDY. Barrage being placed in front of our trenches, Q.6.d.2.0. – R.7.a.9.8. Q.6.c.0.2. and Q.6.a.35.10. 2 guns 4.5" Howitzers on K.36.c.0.2.	CRW
	26.		Lieut. Ramsden proceeded on leave to U.K.	CRW
	29.		At 10.0 pm C/211 came under the orders of Centre Group but remained in its position at Q.22.c.7.7. D/211 (Right Section; came under orders of Lieut. Colonel Birtwistle, commanding Left Group, R.A. 42nd Division Front.	CRW

31.5.17.

Cruickshank Lieut.Colonel.
Commanding 211th Brigade R.F.A.

WAR DIARY
or
INTELLIGENCE SUMMARY

(Erase heading not required.)

Army Form C. 2118.

Place	Date 1917 MAY	Hour	Summary of Events and Information	Remarks and references to Appendices
			Map reference: FRANCE, Sheets, 57c N.E., 57b.S.W., 62c N.E., 62b.N.W., 57c,S.E., 1:40.000", 1:20.000.	CBW
	1.		2nd Lieut. MC IVER R., B/211 returned from Hospital, 30.4.17.	CBW
	2.		Lieut. R.M.GARNETT, rejoined from leave to U.K. and took over his duties as Adjutant. Lieut. Colonel C.E. WALKER, took over tactical command of 211th Brigade R.F.A. from Colonel COLVILLE (Commanding 241st Brigade R.F.A.) and Colonel Lord WYNFORD. (Commenand 240th Brigade). A/211 and B/211 had been attached to 240th Brigade and C/211 and D/211 to 241st Bde.	CBW
	3.		A small operation took place on right of 211th Bde. Front, 211th Brigade Bombarded their S.O.S. line in support of it. CANAL WOOD, OSSUS WOOD. X24.d. a and b - X.30. a. and b.	CBW
	6.		211th Brigade Headquarters moved to E.18.c.4.0.	CBW
	7.		B/211 moved from their position at W.30.c.7.1. and took up a position at X.20.b.4.3. One Section on 7th and Two Sections on 8th.	CBW
	8.		Postings of officers:- 2/Lieut. E.G. FORTH from 42nd L.A.G., No. 2 Section to B/211.	CBW
	9.		2/Lieut. E.G. WALKER from B/211 to No.2 Sect. 42nd D. A. C. Captain S. R. STOTT, C/211, rejoined from leave in U.K.	CBW
	10.		Small Bombardment took place from 3 pm. to 3-15pm to "simulate and attack" 18pdr Batteries fired on their Barrage Line (S.O.S. from the KNOLL F.6.c. to OSSUS WOODY X/30.a.; and on CANAL WOOD, X.18.c. 4.5" How. fired on VENDHUILE.	CBW
	12.		POSTINGS: No. 172. B.S.M. BOWKER, H. B/211 to D/211. No. 453. B.S.M. FINLAY, J. D/211 to B/211.	
	13.		C/211 took part in a bombardment on an enemy trench at A.13.d.8.9. to A.14.a.5.9. The duty of C/211 was to search and sweep 200 yards in rear of this trench, while 4.5" Howitzer (D/210) and 6" Howitzers Bombarded the trench. C/211 registered this trench by means of an Aeroplane before the bombardment commenced.	CBW

Continued/

Vol 5

Confidential.

War Diary.

of

211th Brigade RFA.

From: 1-6-19   To: 30-6-19

Volume II.

WAR DIARY
or
INTELLIGENCE SUMMARY

(Erase heading not required.)

Army Form C. 2118.

Place	Date	Hour	Summary of Events and Information	Remarks and references to Appendices
France	June 2/17		Postings.. 2/Lieut MACKENZIE D.F. From No.2 Sect. D.A.C. to A/2II Battery.	Lost C.
	" 3rd		2/Lieut GIBBS H.B.S. from A/2II Battery to No.2.Sect.D.A.C.	Earl.
			Capt. TRENCH L.C. (Chaplain) rejoined from leave in U.K.	Lost.
	4.6.17		Lieut MACK L.D. A/2II Battery, attached to Bde.H.Q.	
			Personnel from 42nd D.A.C. posted to Brigade as under:—	
			A/2II - 7.O.Ranks. B/2II - 8.O.R nks. H.Q. - 2.O.Ranks	
			C/2II - 3.O.Ranks. D/2II - 4.O.Ranks.	
			Major BROWN D. granted extension of leave to June 2nd. Medical grounds.	
			2 other ranks posted C/2II. 1 other rank posted D/2II.	
			2/Lt SANDYS A.C. A/2II returned from Artillery Course. IV Army School.	
Ref.Map.BIBECOURT. Sheet I	5.6.17		In conjunction with 157 Inf Bde R.F.A. THE following bombardment was carried out—	
1/20,000.			A/2II and C/2II bombarded hostile trench R.I.C 4.8 to Q.6b.2.3.	
			B/2II distributed 5 guns on roads and crater in K.36c. Time 5 to 5.15 p.m. Object. to Nort	
			discover hostile gun positions. Result. Very little retaliation of half hearted nature. Rem.	
			R.A.3554 s/R.S.M.COOMBS W. received ribbon D.C.M. from Div'l.Commander.	
	6.6.17		Lieut.Col. C.E.WALKER received D.S.O. 42nd Div.Arty. Order No.72, d/6.6.17.	
	8.6.17		Major BROWN D. B/2II rejoined from leave.	
			Major NALL J. A/2II rejoined from IV Army Arty School Senior Officers Conference.	
			Lieut. DREWERY G.H. B/2II proceeded on leave to U.K.	
			42nd Div.Soup Kitchen Opened near firing line.	
			Order for all telephone dug-outs to be made gas proof	
			Orders to collect all waste dripping & return to Base for manufacture of glycerine for explos—	
			ives.	
-do-	9.6.17		At 9 p.m. and II p.m. hostile trenches in R.IC, R.Id, & Q6d were bombarded by A/2II,	
			B/2II & C/2II in conjunction with 157th Bde.R.F.A.	
			During the night 8/9th, MINNENWERFER seriously annoyed our infantry in BILHEM Sector.	
			At 4 a.m. 4.5 a.m. & 4.13 a.m. at pre-arranged signal A/2II,B/2II C/2II retaliated on	
			hostile front line in K.36 c and d. while 4.5—in Hows. of 157 Bde. shelled crater K.36.c.A. Lau	
			During night 9/10th 178th Inf.Bde. asked for fire on hostile work in Q.6.a & K.36 c.	
			and between IO p.m. and midnight A/2II, B/2II, & C/2II fired IO section salvos per	
			battery onto this area.	
			At 9.30 p.m. pre-arranged 59th Divn.Arty. bombardment to simulate pending infantry attack	
			participated in by A/2II,B/2II, & C/2II. Area bombarded - hostile firing line in K.36 c & d,	
			lifting to the second line in K.36 a & 7 b.	
			6 a.m. 6.5 a.m. and 6.13 a.m. pre-arranged signal from officers in liaison with the infantry	

WAR DIARY
or
INTELLIGENCE SUMMARY

(Erase heading not required.)

Army Form C. 2118.

Instructions regarding War Diaries and Intelligence Summaries are contained in F. S. Regs., Part II. and the Staff Manual respectively. Title Pages will be prepared in manuscript.

Place	Date	Hour	Summary of Events and Information	Remarks and references to Appendices
	10.6.17		retaliation carried out against MINNENWERFER repeated. During night 10/11th retaliation against MINNENWERFER by A/2II, B/2II & C/2II	
	11.6.17		2/Lieut RAMSDEN N.A. granted extension of leave until 9th June - urgent private affairs. Lieut KESSLER C.E. C/2II struck off strength on evacuation to U.K. sick.	
	12.6.17		2/Lieut CANELISH E.E. posted to C/2II vice Lt. KESSLER C.E. (31.5.17) 2/Lieut RAMSDEN N.A. A/2II returned from leave. Casualties:- I Killed, 8 wounded (4 to hosp. 4 remained on duty) all of B/2II (Shell fire) (10.6.17)	
	13.6.17		Bombardment searching enemy wire and trenches in R.I.b & a carried out by 2II Bde. at 9.45 p.m LL Call received 6.24 p.m. AA Guns firing from L.25a 6.3 Target at once engaged by A/2II,B/2II,C/2II. III Corps bombardment of RIBECOURT 10 p.m. Roads leading in at S.W. corner and crossing town allotted to 2II Bde.	
	14.6.17		Major VALENTINE C.A. D/2II struck off strength as from 2.5.17 on evacuation to U.K. sick. 2/Lieut DALE L.S. struck off strength as from 14.3.17 (evacuated to U.K. sick) Authy. A.F.O 1810 Casualties:- A/2II I other rank. Bullet wound. To hospital. 59th Div. Arty. shelled hostile front line, lifting to the second line in conjunction with remainder of III Corps Artillery, 11.30 p.m. 12.15 a.m. 1 a.m. Three Infantry officers attached to Bde. M. for a few days to get into touch with Artillery work and limitations.	
	16.6.17		Night of 16th & 17th. left Battalion I76 Bde again called for retaliation against MINNENWERFER at 2 a.m. Retaliation on hostile front line in K.36 given by A/2II,B/2II,C/2II. 4 p.m. registration by Aeroplane carried out by A/2II. The visibility of VERY LIGHTS to balloons and back areas was tested noon. Three lights visible to C/2II O.P., Q.17a 3.4.	
	17.6.17		Capt. R.W. BURNYEAT B/2II attached for duty to IV Army Arty School, VAUX.	
	18.6.17		During night 18th/19th, left Battn. I76th Bde asked for fire on road running N from BOAR COPSE. Complied with 3.30 a.m. by A/2II & B/2II. MINNENWERFER suspected of being removed along this road at 3.30 a.m.	
	19.6.17		3rd Section Howitzers, 2/Lt.BUTLER E.R. & 2/Lt ADAMS H.B. and personnel posted to D/2II Bde. from C/298 Bde.R.F.A. Aeroplane Registering for A/2II.	

Army Form C. 2118.

WAR DIARY
or
INTELLIGENCE SUMMARY

(Erase heading not required.)

Instructions regarding War Diaries and Intelligence Summaries are contained in F.S. Regs, Part II. and the Staff Manual respectively. Title Pages will be prepared in manuscript.

Place	Date	Hour	Summary of Events and Information	Remarks and references to Appendices
	20.6.17		Major BOONE H.G. D.S.O. posted to Command D/2II from this date.	
	21.6.17		a/Br ROBERT WILCOX No.71076 B/2II, awarded Military Medal for gallantry and devotion to duty.	
	23.6.17		Lieut H.L KEARNS A/2II returned from leave to U.K.	
	24.6.17		Suspected relief in Bosche lines of 31st I.R. 18 Divn. B/2II joined in 59th Div.Arty bombardment of suspected roads from RIBECOURT during night.24/25.	
	26.6.17		MINNENWERFER heavily shelled 59th Div.Outpost line. At 11 p.m. C/2II fired in retaliation and temporarily silenced the enemy. At 1 a.m. 27th, hostile shelling increased. Retaliation by A/2II,B/2II, & C/2II immediately given. 1.15 a.m. MINNENWERFER silenced.	
	28.6.17		Captain HIGHTON L. (att D/2II) proceeded on 10 days leave to U.K.	
	29.6.17		Suspected relief in Bosche lines of 1st Battn. 86th Inf.Regt. Bombardment of probable route in K.29 carried out by A/2II,B/2II, C/2II.	
			No. T/128319 Dr. W.PAINTER D/2II, sentenced by F.G.C.M. to 90 days F.P. NO.I. Offence— "When Sentry, leaving his post without being properly relieved".	

[signature] for Lieut.colonel.

Commanding 2IIth Brigade R.F.A.

9.6.

Confidential.

War Diary

of

211th Brigade R.F.A.

Volume II.

From: July 1st
To: July 31st 1917.

Army Form C. 2118.

SHEET 1

WAR DIARY
or
INTELLIGENCE SUMMARY

(Erase heading not required.)

Instructions regarding War Diaries and Intelligence Summaries are contained in F.S. Regs, Part II and the Staff Manual respectively. Title Pages will be prepared in manuscript.

Place	Date	Hour	Summary of Events and Information	Remarks and references to Appendices
Reference Map. 57c. N.E. 1:20000.	July 1917 1/2nd		3rd Battalion, 31st I.R. expected to relieve 2nd Battalion L.31.d. and K.36.c., on night 4/5th during the night, 211th Bde., searched all roads other than those suspected as the relief route this was repeated:—	Chw
	3/4th 4/5th		by 157th Bde. on night 2/3rd and on the night 3/4th by 211th Brigade. on night 4/5th. suspected route to trenches heavily shelled by 157th and 211th Brigades R.F.A. 9-30 pm. and 11-15 pm.	Chw Chw
	5/6th 6th		During night A/211 and B/211 harassed hostile Transport in RIBECOURT. No. 705027. B.S.M. Bowker. H. reduced to rank of Sergeant under Section 183 A.A. (III Corps A/80017 dated 6.7.17)	Chw Chw
	6/7th.		No. 705027. Serg. BOWKER, H. posted to A/211. During night A/211 searched roads behind enemy front line. This was repeated by 211th Bde., 3 Batteries, and	Chw Chw
	7/8th 6/7th		3 Batteries, 290th Brigades on night of 7/8th. On account of persistent hostile shelling of B/211, since introduction of the DECAUVILLE line through the Battery Position. One section B/211 withdrew on the night 6/7th to former position Q.13.b.6.3. followed by the remainder of the Battery evening 7/th 8th.	Chw Chw
	9th		Captain G.R. Brown proceeded on leave to U.K. (10 Days). Captain J.F. WARD, R.A.M.C., proceeded on 10 days leave to U.K. Lieut. SHARPIN, R.A.M.C. took over duties of M.O. during absence of Captain Ward. 58th D.A. assumed Tactical and Administration control of 211th Brigade R.F.A. in succession to 59th D.A. for tactics and 42nd D.A. for Administration.	Chw
	10/11th		A strong Patrol of 2/7th London Regt. occupied BOAR COPSE Q.7.c. without opposition. O/211 supplied an extra liaison officer with O.C. 2/7th London's in advanced post Q.6.c. A/211, B/211, C/211, D/211 standing by during occupation of COPSE from which our outposts had been driven previous night.	Chw
	10th.		Lieut. Colonel G.E. WALKER,D.S.O., T.D. proceeded on 14 days leave to U.K. Major BOONE,H.G., D.S.O., D/211 assumed command of 211th Brigade during absence of Lt. Col. WALKER.	Chw
	11th.		Lieut. Parke.T.L. granted extension of leave to 15th inst., by W.O. "Urgent and Private affairs"	Chw
	10th.		Captain.L. HIGHTON, rejoined from leave. D/211 came under Command of 211th Brigade which now becomes Centre Group covering 1 Battalion.	Chw
	11/12th		Centre group joined in 58th D.A. bombardment of Road junction and Railway sidings, K.24.b. L.13.c. and K.23.a. during night.	Chw

2449 Wt. W14957/M90 750,000 1/16 J.B.C. & A. Forms/C.2118/12.

Army Form C. 2118.

SHEET 2

WAR DIARY
INTELLIGENCE SUMMARY

(Erase heading not required.)

Instructions regarding War Diaries and Intelligence Summaries are contained in F.S. Regs., Part II. and the Staff Manual respectively. Title Pages will be prepared in manuscript.

Place	Date 1917	Hour	Summary of Events and Information	Remarks and references to Appendices
	13th 14/15th 15th.		H.Q. 211th Bde. R.F.A. moved from P.18.c.8.5. to Q.15.c.7.3. (1:20000 57d.S.W.) Road and tracks K.21.b., K.29., K.27., engaged by Centre Group. New saps to crater K.34.c. engaged as daily routine programme by centre Group from 15th to 30th July.	Cens Cens
	16th.		Major V. KILVERT, C/211, Captain R.W. BURNYEAT., (4th Army Artillery School VAUX), Captain G.W. Marks, D/211, proceeded on 10 Days leave to U.K. Lieut. C.I. SCOWCROFT, Lieut. R.M. GARNETT, 2/Lieut. GANLISH. E.E., and 2 N.C.O's returned from School of Instruction VAUX.	Cens
	16th/17th		During Evening and night, Patrol Paths, tracts and suspected H.Qs., were subjected to bursts of fire by Centre group; also roads behind Bosche Line. Repeated night 17/18th.	Cens
	18th		5-0pm. Dumps round Ribecourt subjected to concentrated shelling by Centre Group.	Cens
	18th		C/211 heavily shelled for third day. One Gun and water cart knocked out. Orders issued for C/211 to cease fire except in the case of S.O.S. until new position could be occupied. During night 18/19th crashes on road junction fired by 58th L.A. and Bosche front line work harassed by Centre Group.	Cens
	19th.	9-30pm.	174th INFANTRY Brigade asked for retaliation for shelling of Q.4. trenches. 100 rounds fired by Centre Group. During early morning 2-0am. to 4-0am., 20 rounds roads round RIBECOURT.	Cens

WAR DIARY
or
INTELLIGENCE SUMMARY

(Erase heading not required.)

Army Form C. 2118.

SHEET 2

Instructions regarding War Diaries and Intelligence Summaries are contained in F. S. Regs., Part II and the Staff Manual respectively. Title Pages will be prepared in manuscript.

Place	Date 1917	Hour	Summary of Events and Information	Remarks and references to Appendices
PLUSH TRENCH	July 20th		the Bosche new line in R.I. bombarded throughout the day by 4.5. and 6-in Hows. 10.p.m. 10.25 p.m. 20th, and 2 a.m. 21st, Bosche Trench Morter shelled by Centre Group. During night 19th/20th, One Sector C/211 moved to new position in METZ-en-COUTURE.	C/W
	20/21st	10.35 p.m. 20th.	100 Bosches raided our trenches, 175 Inf.Bde. in Q.3 supported by heavy box barrage. The Bosche batteries having shelled Q.3 communication trenches all day. Centre Group immediately put down the S.O.S. barrage, switched over to support the Left Group, firing 1000 rounds between 10.30 and 11.50 p.m. Raid repulsed, and bosches successfully caught in our barrage. C/211 was crossing to new position in METZ during the bombardment.	C/W
	21st.		Capt. C.R.BROWN rejoined for duty from U.K. 706187 Gr Oakden T.D. A/211? wounded in right thigh by shell splinter.	C/W C/W
	21/22nd		One section A/211 occupied position Q.I.a. on PROSPECT HILL, vacated by B/210, remainder of A/211 moving across night 22nd/23rd, and coming under command of LEFT GROUP. During night 21st/22nd single gun of C/211 left behind in former position fired 100 rounds into Bosche outpost works.	C/W
	22/23rd		Dump and Railway sidings in K.23.a. shelled by Centre Group during early morning part of night.	C/W
	23rd 23/24th 24th		Major J NALL rejoined for duty from U.K. proceeded on leave U.K. Junction Road & Railway K.29.b. shelled by Centre Group 23/24th (night) Captain J.F.WARD. (R.A.M.C.) rejoined for duty from U.K. 5.p.m. 24th, 211th Bde. took over Left Group Front in addition to Centre Group A/211 & L/211 rejoining the Brigade, and B/290 & D/290 attached, the six batteries forming Left Group, covering 2 Infantry Brigades. Two night O.P's were instituted in place of previous 1, and Liaison done nightly with 4 Battalions. During the night 24/25th, Trenches and outpost work of the Bosche harassed by A/211, B/211, C/211, & D/211.	C/W C/W
	25th.		Lieut.Col.C.M.WALKER.D.S.O. rejoined Brigade from U.K. and resumed Command of 211th Bde. Batteries instructed to select single gun positions from which all firing other than S.O.S. to be done. Seven positions known as pirates were selected, camouflaged, and surveyed by survey Co. During night 25th/26th, roads behind Bosche line shelled by B/211, and B/290. 175th Infantry Bde. arranged to raid snipers posts & T.M. emplacements K.33.d. L/211 shelled elephant huts K.33.d. during the afternoon and A/211 & C/211 put down covering barrage of shrapnel during raid 10.33 p.m.	C/W

WAR DIARY
or
INTELLIGENCE SUMMARY

(Erase heading not required.)

Army Form C. 2118.

SHEET 4

Place	Date 1917	Hour	Summary of Events and Information	Remarks and references to Appendices
	July 26th		Early morning 26th inst. 175th Brigade asked for fire on Bosege patrol 400 yards from our line. C/2II put over 15 rounds. Major H.G.BOONE D.S.O. rejoined L/2II and resumed command.	CMW
	27th		During night 26th/27th, Left Group fired 500 rounds into HAVRINCOURT. Evening of the 27th, test of S.O.S. rockets carried out on 58th Division front. During night, Left Group fired 200 rounds into roads N.E. of HAVRINCOURT. Captain L.HIGHTON posted to L/2IO but remains with L/2II at discretion of C.O. 2IO Bde. R.F.A. (42 R.A.Order No I30.)	CMW
	28th		173rd Inf.Bde. carried out raid on PLUSH TRENCH R.I. at 12.45 a.m. B/290 putting down barrage (shrapnel) and L/290 blocking support trench. 9.30 p.m. and 10.30 p.m. Left Group bombarded Dump and Railway siding K.23.a. for 30 seconds. Lieut SCOWCROFT C.I. proceeded on 10 days leave to U.K. 27.7.17.	CMW
	29th		Communications in K.29 harassed by 58th D.A. furing night. Lieut G.A.S. COLLIN proceeded on Successors course at 4th Army Arty.School. VAUX. e/Lt L.F.MACKENZIE " " " " " "	CMW
	28th		Lieut W.N. HOUGH. attached to H.Q. vice Lieut. G.A.S. COLLIN. 174th Inf.Bde. relieved by 1st South African Brigade. C/2II S.O.S. Lines altered for night 28th/29th only as precaution against suspected raid. During afternoon 28th, heavy T.M. shelling of Q.3 trenches finally silenced by L/2II and A/2II. 174th Inf Bde. sent word of thanks.	CMW
	30th		Night O.P. established on high ground in middle of Left Group zone Q.9.a. use of the other night O.P's. being discontinued. Captain G.W.MARKS & Lieut F.KNOWLES rejoined for duty from U.K.	CMW
	31st		C.R.A. 9th Division assumed control Left Group. During early morning 30th inst., roads round RIBECOURT bombarded. During night 31st/1st, trench system and suspected Hdqrs. S.E. of HAVRINCOURT shelled by Left Group 500 rounds.	CMW

Aug 1st/1917

Clundeker Lieut. Colonel.

Commanding 2IIth Brigade R.F.A.

Vol 7

Confidential.

War Diary.
of
211th Brigade R.F.A (T).

From Aug 1/17.
To Aug 31/17.

Army Form C. 2118.

WAR DIARY
or
INTELLIGENCE SUMMARY
(Erase heading not required.)

Instructions regarding War Diaries and Intelligence Summaries are contained in F. S. Regs, Part II and the Staff Manual respectively. Title Pages will be prepared in manuscript.

Place	Date 1917	Hour	Summary of Events and Information	Remarks and references to Appendices
	AUGUST			
	1.		2/Lieut. J.T.FOTHEOARY, D/211 and 2/Lieut. LOWTHER, G. to 34th Brigade R.F.A.	Cw
	2.		211th Brigade moved to positions in GOUZEAUCOURT WOOD handing over own guns and positions 9th Divisional Artillery and taking over those of 58th Divisional Artillery.	Cw
	4.		40th Divisional Artillery assumed tactical control of 211th Brigade R.F.A.	Cw
	6.		Major BOONE.H.G. on 10 days to United Kingdom. Major NALL.J. and Major KILVERT.V. returned from leave in United Kingdom.	Cw Cw
	10.		Lieut. MACK.L.D. on 10 days leave to United Kingdom. Lieut. MACK.L.D. Adjutant dated 17/6/17 vice Lieut. GARNETT R.M.resigned. Lieut SOOWCROFT.G.from leave to United Kingdom.	Cw
	14. 16. 17.		Lieut. MACK. L.D. to be A/Captain while holding appointment of Adjutant. a/Captain MACK L.D. to Brigade Hdqs from A/211 Lieut GARNETT R.M. posted to A/211 Major BOONE.H.D.D.S.O. from leave in United Kingdom.	
	19.		Lieut. SANDYS A.C. from 10days leave in United Kingdom.	
			MENTIONED IN DESPATCHES.	
	20.		For Sinai Peninsular October 1916 - February 1917: Lieut.Col. C.E. WALKER.D.S.O. T.D. 211th Brigade; Capt. Highton.L. late 42nd D.A.C. No. 3554. B.S.M. Coombs.W. 14H. B.S.M. Lee. E. 211th Brigade.	Cw
	22.		211th Brigade evacuated positions sending one section per battery to wagon Lines night 21/22nd remainder night 22/23rd.	
	23.		Capt. L.D. MACK. from 10 days leave in United Kingdom. Lieut .G.W. MARKS to be Captain 1/6/16.	
	25.		211th Brigade route marched to PERONNE and there entrained for GODEWAERSVELDE.	
	26.		Detrained GODEWAERSVELDE marched to WATOU and there encamped.	

Army Form C. 2118.

WAR DIARY
or
INTELLIGENCE SUMMARY

(Erase heading not required.)

Instructions regarding War Diaries and Intelligence Summaries are contained in F. S. Regs., Part II and the Staff Manual respectively. Title Pages will be prepared in manuscript.

Place	Date 1917	Hour	Summary of Events and Information	Remarks and references to Appendices
	AUGUST			
	28.		One section per battery went into action East of Ypres relieving 15th D.A. Artillery.	(Enc)
	29.		Remainder of Batteries and Hdqrs took over from 15th D.A. Lieut. Col. C.H. WALKER D.S.O. assumed command of 15th D.A. Rt. sub-group consisting of 210th Bde, 211th Bde and 14th Australian F.A. Bde. Bombardment of area South of Zevenkote maintained day and night during 29th by Rt. Sub. Group.	CRW
	30.		Bombardment continued at varied times of day and night.	(En)
	31.		Bombardment continued. Hun replied wounding 7 men 211th Brigade and gassing one. Lieut. MACKENZIE, L.F. on 10 days leave to United Kingdom. Major BURNEBA T. B.W. B/211 transferred to 23rd Div. Arty. ATTACHMENTS. Capt. G.W. MARKS from D/211 to 42nd D.A.C. Lieut. G.A.S. GOLLIN from Hdqrs. to D/211. Lieut. R.M. GARNETT from A/211 to Hdqrs.	CRW

CONFIDENTIAL

WAR DIARY

of

211th Bde R.F.A.

From 1-9-17 to 30-9-17

Vol VII

WAR DIARY
INTELLIGENCE SUMMARY
(Erase heading not required.)

Army Form C. 2118.

Instructions regarding War Diaries and Intelligence Summaries are contained in F.S. Regs., Part II. and the Staff Manual respectively. Title pages will be prepared in manuscript.

Place	Date	Hour	Summary of Events and Information	Remarks and references to Appendices
			ADMINISTRATIVE	
	SEPTEMBER 1917			
	4		Posting. No 16432 R.S.M. Minchin W. posted from Base	z.9.9.
	11		Leave. 2 Lt McIver on leave to U.K. 11 days.	z.9.9.
	9		Attachment Capt G. W. Martos to No I Sect. D.A.C. 42nd Div.	z.9.9.
	11		Posting. R.S.M. Coombs to B.211 as B.S.M.	z.9.9.
	13		Arrival. Lt McKenzie from 10 days leave to U.K.	z.9.9.
	18		O.C. Lt: Col: E.J. Inches. DSO assumed command of 211th Bde R.F.A.	z.9.9.
	19		Posting. Major W.J. Highett to D.211 to command.	z.9.9.
	28		Rest Camp Lt T.L. Parke and 14 ORs to V Army Rest Camp (12 days)	z.9.2.
	29		Reinforcement 72 ORs. from Base through D.A.C. posted as under	z.9.2.
			A.211 16, B.211 14, C.211 22, D.211 20.	
			Casualties during September	

	Killed		Wounded		Gassed		
	O	ORs	O	ORs	O	ORs	
H.Qs.						8	
A.211		4	1	13	2	15	
B.211		2		14		16	
C.211		1		9		10	
D.211	2	-	2	4		27	
	2	7	3	40	4	76	

Names of officers & dates of casualty.

Sept: 5 Major H.G. Boone. D.S.O. Wounded (died Sept 16)
     "   Lieut   W.N. Hough.   "   shell.
     9 Lt.Col. C.E. Walker. D.S.O. Gas.
     10 2Lt   A.L. Makinson.   "
     " Major D. Brown   "
     25 Lieut   J. Almond   shell.
     "   N.A. Ramsden.   shell.
     29 Major W.T. Highet. M.C. shell shock + wounds
     " 2Lieut E. Butler.   killed.   g.9.9.

Army Form C. 2118.

Army Form C. 2118.

WAR DIARY
INTELLIGENCE SUMMARY.
(Erase heading not required.)

Instructions regarding War Diaries and Intelligence Summaries are contained in F. S. Regs., Part II. and the Staff Manual respectively. Title pages will be prepared in manuscript.

Place	Date	Hour	Summary of Events and Information TACTICAL	Remarks and references to Appendices
	SEPTEMBER 1917			
	1-5		Area searches carried out by 211th Bde. 42nd D.A. assumed control.	? ? ?
	6		Lanes Fusiliers attacked Hun front line & strong points on a front of 1 mile. Creeping and protective barrage put down by 211th Bde. Infantry failed to reach objectives.	? ? ?
	9		Lt. Col. Ad Birtwistle assumed tactical command of group	? ? ?
	10-19		Heavy area searches repeated daily	? ? ?
	16			? ? ?
	20		9th D.A. assumed control of Ypres sector	? ? ?
			In conjunction with divisions on right & left 9th attacked and captured enemy front line & strong points to a depth of 1 mile. - 211th Bde participated in 24 hours previous bombardment followed by creeping and protective barrage.	
	21		3rd D.A. assumed control of Ypres sector	? ? ?
	22		One section per battery moved up into position behind FREZENBERG RIDGE but remained out of action.	? ? ?
	23		Remainder of batteries moved up into forward position	? ? ?
	24		Batteries came into action	? ? ?
	26		3rd Division in conjunction with flank divisions attacked and captured enemy front line and strong points to a depth of 1000 yds. 211th Brigade participated in bombardment & creeping & protective barrage.	? ? ?
	27		Big Hun counter attack repulsed.	? ? ?

WAR DIARY

INTELLIGENCE SUMMARY

Army Form C. 2118.

Place	Date	Hour	Summary of Events and Information	Remarks and references to Appendices
	SEPTEMBER 1917		TACTICAL	
	28		One section per battery relieved by one section 3rd N.Z. Bde. Hun counter attack repulsed.	? ? ?
	29		Remainder of batteries relieved by 3rd N.Z. Brigade	? ? ?
	30		2/II Bde marched from Wagon Lines to WORMHOUDT	? ? ?

E. J. Grener
Lt Col comdg
2/II Bde R.F.A.

Vol 9

Confidential

War Diary
of
211th Brigade RFA

From October 1st to October 31st

Vol VIII

WAR DIARY
INTELLIGENCE SUMMARY

Army Form C. 2118.

(Erase heading not required.)

Place: In the Field

Date 1917	Hour	Summary of Events and Information	Remarks and references to Appendices
		Maps 1/40,000 FURNES. Prov: Issue 1/40,000 TETEGHEM area	
OCTOBER			
1		MOVE Brigade trekked from WORMHOUDT to TETEGHEM area	
2		" Brigade trekked from TETEGHEM area to LA PANNE	
		Relief. Night 2/3 a section of each battery relieved 331 Bde. (66th Div.)	
3		" Night 3/4 remainder of batteries moved in.	
4		" Command passed to O.C. 211th Bde (Lt.Col. INCHES) at 5.30 A.M.	
		POSTINGS Officers. Lieut. E. FORTH to B211 2/10/17	
		" A.C. SANDYS. to D211 from A211	
		" Hospital 2 Lieut. F.A. MOOLENAAR C211. To hospital, gassed.	
5		SIGNALLING CLASS 3 ORs to Divisional Signal School.	
		POSTING 2 Lieut. F.T. BLENNERHASSETT to 211th Bde. C211.	
6		POSTING Capt. C.R. BROWN. A211 to command D211 2/10/17	
		" F. STOTT C211 to command B211 2/10/17	
		" Lieut. C.I. SCOWCROFT D211 to A211 2/10/17	
		" R.M. GARNETT. A211 to HQs 2/10/17	
		" H.W.L. KEARNS. attached to HQs RA	
7		DEPARTURES Mons: DUPRES. interpr.(?) 211th Bde reported for duty at FRENCH MISSION	
8		Lieut. L. PARKE B211 on leave to UK from V Army Rest Camp BOULOGNE (DUNKERQUE)	
		POSTINGS Capt. G.W. MARKS to No.1 Section DAC	
		Lieut. BLENNERHASSETT from C211 to D211	
9/9		COURSE CAMOUFLAGE. Lt. F.J.G. JACKSON.	
10		REST CAMP 8 ORs (2 per Battery) to Rest Camp XV Corps.	
11		RELIEF night of 11/12 one section each battery was relieved by 410th Division and itself relieved 32nd in R. Division Area	

E.J. Inches
Lt.Col.

Army Form C. 2118.

WAR DIARY
or
INTELLIGENCE SUMMARY
(Erase heading not required.)

Instructions regarding War Diaries and Intelligence Summaries are contained in F.S. Regs., Part II. and the Staff Manual respectively. Title Pages will be prepared in manuscript.

Sheet 1.

Place	Date 1917	Hour	Summary of Events and Information	Remarks and references to Appendices
In the Field	OCTOBER 12		ARRIVAL Lieut H.W.L. KEARNS. A.211 Returned from HQs R.A.	2.9.9.
	13		RELIEF night 12/13 Remainder of Batteries moved.	2.9.9.
			COMMAND passed at 12 noon.	
			LEAVE Capt TRENCH. A.E. on 4 days leave BOULOGNE	
	14		ARRIVAL Lieut J. ALMOND from hospital. POSTING 2Lieut F.T. BLENNERHASSETT B.211 to C.211	2.9.9.
			DEPARTURES Course Lieut C.I. SEONCROFT + 3 ORs to DIV. GAS SCHOOL	2.9.9.
	15		B.211 One gun badly smashed by hostile shelling.	2.9.9.
	16		BOMBARDMENT PALACE HOTEL WESTENDE BAINS was heavily shelled by orders of CORPS. D.211 only taking part, B.211 Bttle. ~~the~~	2.9.9. 2.9.9.
	15		REST CAMP 18 ORs to XV CORPS REST CAMP	2.9.9.
	17		STRUCK OFF Major HIGHET. D.211 having been evacuated to UK.	2.9.9.
			POSTINGS. From BASE } 2Lieut CROLL. S.A. 2Lieut CRYER.W.N. A.211. 2Lieut TALBOT.A.W. A.211 Through D.A.C }	2.9.9.
	18		STRUCK OFF Lieut RAMSDEN. N.A. Evacuated to UK.	2.9.9.
			DRAFT 37 ORs from RH and RFA Base.	
			COURSES CAMOUFLAGE. Lieut G.A.S. COLLIN	
			HONOURS MILITARY MEDAL. 705 325 Sgt HALLORAN. A.211 705414 Bdr ASHTON A.211 710 247 Bdr WADDINGTON. A.211 705 470 Gnr HARGREAVES A.211 695072 Gnr COUPE A.211 443932 Pnr BELLAMY HQs. 443928 " WILKINSON. HQs.	2.9.9.
	20		HONOURS MILITARY CROSS Capt. The Revd A.C. TRENCH. C.F	2.9.9.

Army Form C. 2118.

WAR DIARY
INTELLIGENCE SUMMARY
(Erase heading not required.)

Place: In the Field

Place	Date	Hour	Summary of Events and Information	Remarks and references to Appendices
	OCTOBER 1917			
	22		ARRIVALS Lieut. R. McIVER. from leave to UK	A.9.9.
			Major D. BROWN from BASE to B211 to command	A.9.9.
	23		LEAVE Lieut. F.J.G. JACKSON, C.211. 10 days to UK.	A.9.9.
			POSTINGS Capt. S.R. STOTT from B211 to C211	A.9.9.
	26		LEAVE 2 Lieut: F.A. MOOLENAAR granted 21 days sick leave.	A.9.9.
	27		DRAFT 16 ORs from BASE RHQ RFA.	A.9.9.
			POSTING Lieut BREWRY from B211 to A211	A.9.9.
	30		LEAVE Lieut T.L. PARKE granted 1 month's leave to UK	A.9.9.
	31		COURSE Lieut D.F. MACKENZIE + 2 ORs to Div: Gas School.	A.9.9.
	30		HONOUR MILITARY MEDAL. 710279 Gnr KEIGHLEY. M. B211	A.9.9.
			CASUALTIES IN OCTOBER	
			Officers.	
			2 Lieut F.A. MOOLENAAR Wounded. Gas	
			Other Ranks	
			Killed Wounded Missing	
			Shell. Gas	
			7 12 18 2	

E.J. Snelson
Lt RFC
Comm. 211 Bde
R.F.A.

WAR DIARY.

of

211th Bde R.F.A

From 1-11-17
To   30-11-17.

Vol VIII

WAR DIARY.

211TH. BRIGADE, R.F.A.   NOVEMBER. 1917.

1	Course	LT. F. KNOWLES to 13th. Vety. School. Three O.R. to Div. Gas School.	
2	Posting	LT. F.T.BLENNERHASSET from B.211 to C.211.	
3	Posting	Six O.R. from Base Depot.	
	Course	LT. F.T.BLENNERHASSET & 4 ON.C.O.s to 4th. Army Arty. Three O.R. to Ordnance, one O.R. to 15th. CMDS(School)	
4	Course	LT. W.N.CRYER to to 4th. Army Artillery School.	
5	Appointment.	CAPT.C.R.BROWN to be A/MAJOR with effect from 16.10.17. LT. C.I.SCOWCROFT to be A/CAPT with effect from 16.10.17	
	Leave	LT. E.Forth on 14 days' leave to the U.K.	
	Award	44427 Pnr. J.Buttle awarded the MILITARY MEDAL.	
8	Course	MAJOR J.NALL to Shoeburyness on Artillery Course. CAPT. S.R.STOTT to Shoeburyness on Artillery Course. CAPT. TRENCH to Boulogne on Chaplains' Course.	
14	Leave	L.T.L.PARKE granted 6 months leave with effect 15.10.17	
	Strength	LT. F.A.MOLENAAR evacuated to the U.K. and struck off the strength	
16	Awards	710313 Dvr E. Greenwood &B211 awarded MILITARY MEDAL 710087 Gnr. Baines B211 awarded MILITARY MEDAL	
17	Award	LT. K.MACIVER awarded the MILITARY CROSS. 133rd	
19	Movement	Night 19/20 Half of each Battery relieved by FRENCH D.A	
20	"	Night 20/21 Remainder of Bde. relieved by FRENCH D.A	
21	"	Evening. Brigade marched to GHYVELDE.	
23	"	Brigade marched from GHYVELDE to WORMHOUDT.	
	Course	MAJOR C.R.BROWN to Shoeburyness for Artillery Course. CAPT. G.A.S.COLLIN to Shoeburyness for Artillery Course	
	Transfer	LT.A.W.TALBOT transferred to Base Depot(DGMS GHQ 445/1)	
	Leave	LT. J.AIMOND on 14 days' leave to the U.K.	
24	Movement	Brigade marched to REITVELD.	
	Leave	LT. J.R.TOMMIS on 14 days' leave to the U.K.	
25	Movement	Brigade marched to HAZEBROUCK.	
26	"	Brigade marched to XXXXXX FONTES.	
28	Award	LT. F.J.G.JACKSON awarded the MILITARY CROSS.	
30	Movement	Brigade marched to CALONNE.	
		Night 30/1 One Section C.211, one Section D.211 relieved corresponding Sections of 25th. D.A. in action at FESTUBERT. PORTUGUESE Army on left flank, 46th Div. on right flank.	

E. J. Inches
Lt-Col Comdg
211 Bde R.F.A.

Vol II

CONFIDENTIAL

WAR DIARY

of

211th Brigade, R.F.A.

From 1st December, 1917 to 31st December, 1917.

VOLUME II

211TH
F.A. BRIGADE,
R.F.A.

WAR DIARY
or
INTELLIGENCE SUMMARY.

(Erase heading not required.)

Army Form C. 2118.

211TH F.A. BRIGADE, R.F.A.

Place	Date 1917 Dec	Hour	Summary of Events and Information	Remarks and references to Appendices
	1		A.211 marched from ROBECQ to ESSARS X.25 d 1.9 & there handed over 6 18pdr. guns to 25 D.A. B.211 marched from ROBECQ to ESSARS X.19 c 1.8, handed over three guns to 25th D.A., and with remaining 3 guns relieved 5 guns 25th. D.A. in action near FESTUBERT F.4 d 2.8 Remaining 4 guns C.211 relieved 4 guns 25th. D.A. in action near FESTUBERT X.30 c 5.5 D.211 with 4 Hows. relieved 4 Hows. 25th. D.A. in action near FESTUBERT F. 6 a. Hqrs. 211th. Bde. relieved Hqrs. 112th. Bde. at LOISNE X. 28 a. and became Left Group, having C.210 attached. Portuguese on our left. 46 Division on Right.	
	2		Enemy's defenses in LA BASSEE area registered.	
	3		Strengthening Battery positions commenced. Lieut. G.H. DREWRY attached to Headquarters as Signal Officer.	
	4		Captain S.R. STOTT posted to XIII Corps (autzy. 42nd Div. Wire A.35/6/47 dated 2.12.17.	
	5.		Lieut. H.W.L. KEARNS posted to Headquarters 42nd Div. Arty.	
	8.		Night O.P. party for S.O.S. Rocket observation installed in GIRLS' SCHOOL FESTUBERT. Lieut-Colonel E.J. INCHES. proceeded to AMIENS for course of Aerial observation. Lieut. GILLIATT 4th Squad. R.F.C. attd. to Bde. Headquarters for Artillery observation. Lieut. A.E. DYKE proceeded to First Army Artillery School. Lieut. F. KNOWLES proceeded to Shoeburyness on Artillery Course for Senior Officers. Major D. BROWN assumed temporary command during absence of Lieut-Colonel IN CHES.	
	8-14			
	9		Wire cutting by 18 pdrs. started in A.3.c. A.211 personnel relieve C.211 personnel in the line. Wire-cutting included in daily routine Lieut. R.M.GARNETT rejoined A.211 from Headquarters. Position of Orderly Officer restored to establishment. Lieut. G.H. DREWRY posted to Bde. H.Qrs. and assumed duties of Orderly Officer.	
	10.		Lieut. J.K.GRANT and 7 o.r. proceeded to 42nd Div. Sig. School. Lieut. R.P.KNOWLES appointed acting Captain vice Captain S.R.STOTT (A.A. & QMG A 7/1077)	

Army Form C. 2118.

WAR DIARY
or
INTELLIGENCE SUMMARY
(Erase heading not required.)

Instructions regarding War Diaries and Intelligence Summaries are contained in F. S. Regs., Part II. and the Staff Manual respectively. Title pages will be prepared in manuscript.

211th F.A. BRIGADE R.F.A.

Place	Date 1917 DEC	Hour	Summary of Events and Information	Remarks and references to Appendices
	11		Major V. KILVERT proceeded to AMIENS for Aerial observation course. Lieut. DAVIS 4th Squad. R.F.C. attd. to Bde. Hqrs. for Artillery observation.	
	12		D.211 took over one 4"5" Howitzer from 46th D.A. bringing it into action at the main position F.6.a.	
	13		Salvoes on roads and tracks by 18 pdrs. and shelling of new work by 4"5" Hows. adopted as nightly programme.	
	14		Alternative positions for each Battery selected - repairs on these positions begun. Lieut. F.J.G. JACKSON proceeded to AMIENS for course of Aerial observation.	
	15		Points in enemy's defenses selected for aerial registration and forwarded to R.F.C. Lieut. (a/Capt.) C.I. SCOWCROFT promoted Captain with precedence from 1.6.1916. Lieut. (a/Capt.) M.F. THOMPSON promoted Captain with precedence from 1.6.1916. Lieut. RHODES posted to D.211 from D.A.C.	
	17		Major W.T. HIGHETT M.C. mentioned in despatches London Gazette 11.12.17. Lieut. F. KNOWLES mentioned in despatches London Gazette 11.12.17.	
	18		Rear positions for occupation in the case of hostile advance reconnoitred for all Batteries.	
	19		Personnel C.211 relieved personnel A.211 in action. Personnel A.211 relieved personnel B.211 who withdrew to Wagon lines. Lieut. L.BUCK posted to D.211 from B.210.	
	20		Placing of barbed wire round battery positions begun. B.211 begin course of Musketry. Position reconnoitred for anti-tank gun. Policy adopted of retaliating for hostile fire in the proportion of 2 to 1.	
	21		18 pdrs. ordered to stop wire-cutting which is taken over by 4"5" Hows.	
	22		1411 B.S.M. LEE E. awarded D.C.M. London Gazette November 26th 1917. Major J. NALL gave a lecture to Officers (Artillery Course Sheeburyness)	

WAR DIARY
INTELLIGENCE SUMMARY.
(Erase heading not required.)

Army Form C. 2118.

Place	Date 1917 Dec	Hour	Summary of Events and Information	Remarks and references to Appendices
	24	a.m.	Special routine of concentrations on selected enemy points carried out. Evening. D.211 fired gas shell concentration, and 18 pdrs. H.E. concentration in conformation to 42nd Div. scheme.	
	26		O.Ps. for rear positions reconnoitred. B.211 received two guns from I.O.M. and took over three from A.211. They came into action F.5.b.5.3. near FESTUBERT. A.211 received four guns and brought them into action F.4.d.2.8. at the same time taking over the detached section of B.211 in X.24.a. D.211 received one 4"5 How. from I.O.M. and brought it into action at F.6.a.	
	27th		1 Section D.211 retire to position E.5.c. as battery position was considered to advanced. C.211 personnel W.L. trained in Musketry. 2/Lieutenants P.W. STEVENS. A.211; H. TOPPING B.211; B.A. BLACKBOROW C.211; J.P. HEYWORTH D.211, and J.A. LECHERTIER A.211; posted from Base Depot.	
	28		Remainder D.211 retire to position E.5.c. Lieut. G.H. DREWRY proceeded to Div. Arty. Headquarters to attend CAMOUFLAGE Course.	
	29		200 rounds fired in retaliation for enemy shelling GIVENCHY.	
	30		Lieut. A.E. BURTWISTLE proceeded to Div. Gas School.	
	31		C.211 W.L. personnel have use of Rifle range.	

	KILLED	WOUNDED	Attended COURSES	LEAVE in U.K.
Officers.		1	6	1
O.R.	1	1	28	8

Army Form C. 2118.

9/12

WAR DIARY
INTELLIGENCE SUMMARY.
(Erase heading not required.)

CONFIDENTIAL

WAR DIARY

of

211th. Brigade R.F.A.

From 1st. January 1918 to 31st. January 1918

VOLUME III.

Place	Date	Hour	Summary of Events and Information	Remarks and references to Appendices

Instructions regarding War Diaries and Intelligence Summaries are contained in F. S. Regs., Part II. and the Staff Manual respectively. Title pages will be prepared in manuscript.

Army Form C. 2118.

WAR DIARY
INTELLIGENCE SUMMARY.
(Erase heading not required.)

Instructions regarding War Diaries and Intelligence Summaries are contained in F. S. Regs., Part II. and the Staff Manual respectively. Title pages will be prepared in manuscript.

Place	Date	Hour	Summary of Events and Information	Remarks and references to Appendices
	1918 January			
	1		Personnel one section A.211 withdrawn to Wagon Line for musketry instruction- Frost prevents any concrete work. "Y" Bty.Medium T.M., and one mortar of "V" Heavy T.M., grouped with LEFT GROUP (A.211, B.211, C.211, D.211, and B.210) for tactical purposes. Plan of communications for four reinforcing batteries drawn up and O.Ps. reconnoitred	
	2		Personnel of A.211 Wagon Line passed through gas school to test respirators.	
	3		Night firing discontinued. Targets arranged with No. 2 Squadron R.F.C. for registration. Destructive shoot on C.211 carried out by two 15cm. Hows. Result gun carriage and trail damaged, 4 gun pits destroyed. Shoot directed by E.O.B. Lieut. G.H.DREWRY returned from Div. Camouflage Course	
	4		Aeroplane registration carried out by 6" T.M. C.211 withdrew from position X.30. C.5.3 and come into action F.5.c.0.3. Lieut R.M.GARNETT proceeded to the U.K. on 14 days' leave. 2/Lt.H.Topping transferred from B.211 to D.211, and 2/Lt. J.P.Heyworth from D.211 to B.211.	
	5		Positions reconnoitred for 8 reinforcing batteries, making 12 reinforcing positions in all. Rear positions and rear O.Ps. to cover 2nd. line system reconnoitred for eight reinforcing batteries. Orders received to restrct firing to sniping movements and responses to Infantry calls in order to quieten front in accordance with the Defensive Policy. Lieut.-Colonel E.J.INCHES visited 42nd, Divisional Wing to inspect musketry and physical drill classes supplied from 42nd D.A.Brigades.	
	6		2/Lt. A.B.DYKE A.211 arrived from 1st. Army Artillery School.	
	7		Thaw begins. Lieut J.K.GRANT and 2/Lt. J.R.RHODES arrive from Div. Signal School. Lieut A.E.Birtwistle arrives from the Div. Gas School Lieut K.MACIVER proceeded to 1st. Army Artillery School	

Army Form C. 2118.

WAR DIARY
INTELLIGENCE SUMMARY.
(Erase heading not required.)

Instructions regarding War Diaries and Intelligence Summaries are contained in F. S. Regs., Part II. and the Staff Manual respectively. Title pages will be prepared in manuscript.

Place	Date 1917	Hour	Summary of Events and Information	Remarks and references to Appendices
	January 6	4 p.m. and 5 p.m.	Hostile H.T.M. bombarded our trenches between the LA BASSEE Road and the CANAL. LEFT GROUP co-operated in D.A. and H.A. retaliation on T.M. and H.QRS. in hostile area.	W/o
	8		O.Ps. of C.211 and B.211 interchanged. Advanced party 84th. A.F.A.Bde reconnoitred four of the LEFT GROUP reinforcing positions. Track for Decauville to C.211 position reconnoitred. Heavy snowfall. Personnel one section D.211 withdraw to Wagon Line for musketry. Personnel section A.211 return into action. Construction of miniature rifle ranges at gun positions and Wagon Lines begun.	W/o
	9		Captain G.A.S.COLLIN arrived from B Battery Commanders' Course. U.K. Major C.R.BROWN D.211 posted to command A.170th. Bde R.F.A. Major L.HIGHTON D.210 posted to command D.211 vice Major C.R.BROWN.	W/o
	10		Advanced parties of 84th. Bde. arrived and occupied positions. 2/Lt. W.N.CRYER rejoined A.211 from B.211.	W/o
	11		Captain J.F.WARD and Lieut D.F.Mackenzie proceeded on 7 days' leave to PARIS.	W/o
	12		2/Lt. L.BUCK D.211 posted to 42nd. Div. Ammn. Col. Lieut. J.J.COWIESON D.211 posted from D.A.C.	W/o
	13		Capt. M.F. THOMPSON proceeded on 14 days' leave to U.K.	W/o
	15.		R.S.M. W.MUNCHIN posted to 41st. D.A.C. and B.S.M. E.LEE A.211 became Temporary R.S.M. of 211th. Bde.	W/o
	17		Lieut F.T.BLENNERHASSET C.211 proceeded on Mining Course at HOUCHIN. Major V.KILVERT proceeded to U.K. on Battery Commanders' Course.	W/o
	18.		2/Lt.A.E.MACIVER LINGO HOSPITAL SICK 2/Lt. K. MACIVER to hospital – sick.	W/o

Army Form C. 2118.

WAR DIARY
INTELLIGENCE SUMMARY.
(Erase heading not required.)

Instructions regarding War Diaries and Intelligence Summaries are contained in F. S. Regs., Part II, and the Staff Manual respectively. Title pages will be prepared in manuscript.

Place	Date 1918	Hour	Summary of Events and Information	Remarks and references to Appendices
	January 18		Capt. G.A.S.COLLIN assumed temporary command of C.211 vice Major V.KILVERT. 2/Lt. A.B.DYKE transferred from A.211 to B.211.	
	20		Lieut. R.M.GARNETT arrived from 14 days' leave in U.K. Capt. J.F.WARD and Lieut D.F.MACKENZIE returned from 7 days' leave in PARIS. 2/Lt. A.W.J.TALBOT posted to A.211 from Base Depot.	
	21		Lieut A.E.BIRTWISTLE proceeded on 14 days' leave to U.K.	
	22		Capt. F.KNOWLES arrived from Battery Commanders' Course in U.K.	
	23		B.84 and C.84 move into action, B.84 at X.22.d. C.84 at F.10.d.9.4. Reinforcing positions for 4 batteries begun. Lecture given by Capt. COLLIN on Overseas Course Subjects. Capt. C.I.SCOWCROFT proceeded on 7 days' leave to PARIS. Lt. MARSHALL attached to C.211 from Div. Hqrs. 2/Lt. M.G.WELLS posted to C.211 from Base Depot.	
	24		D.211 carry out registration with aeroplane observation.	
	24		Lecture given by Major HIGHTON on Overseas Course Subjects. Normal traffic resumed on roads.	
	26		84th Bde Hqrs. took over command of LEFT GROUP from Hqrs. 211th. Bde. Hqrs. 211th.Bde. moved to LOCON. Lieut.-Col. E.J.INCHES proceeded on Senior Officers' Course to U.K. Major J.NALL assumed temporary command of 211th Bde. Lieut J.ALMOND proceeded to AMIENS for Aerial Observation Course.	
	27		Lieut G.H.DREWRY proceeded to U.K.on 14 days' leave	
	28		2/Lt. J.R.RHODES proceeded to WIMEREUX for Camouflage Course.	

WAR DIARY
INTELLIGENCE SUMMARY.
(Erase heading not required.)

Army Form C. 2118.

Place	Date	Hour	Summary of Events and Information	Remarks and references to Appendices
	1918 January 30		Captain M.F.THOMPSON arrived from 14 days' leave in U.K.	
	31		Capt. C.I.SCOWCROFT arrived from 7 days' leave to PARIS. 2/Lt. J.R.RHODES arrived from Camouflage Course. Capt. J.WADDELL proceeded on 14 days' leave to the United Kingdom.	

SUMMARY

	ARRIVALS		DEPARTURES	
	O.	R.	O.	R.
Leave	5	20	7	48
Hospital	1	15	1	39
Postings	4	24	2	15
Courses	7	28	7	35

Promotions   24 O.Rs.

Murray
Capt
for Major

Andy. 2/1 Bn KRRF

Army Form C. 2118.

211TH F.A. BRIGADE R.F.A.
No 542/84
1. iii. 18.

Vol 13

WAR DIARY
or
INTELLIGENCE SUMMARY.
(Erase heading not required.)

Instructions regarding War Diaries and Intelligence Summaries are contained in F. S. Regs., Part II. and the Staff Manual respectively. Title pages will be prepared in manuscript.

CONFIDENTIAL.

WAR DIARY

of

211th. Brigade R.F.A.

From 1st. January 1918. to 28th. February 1918.

VOLUME III

Place	Date	Hour	Summary of Events and Information	Remarks and references to Appendices

Army Form C. 2118.

WAR DIARY
or
INTELLIGENCE SUMMARY.
(Erase heading not required.)

Instructions regarding War Diaries and Intelligence Summaries are contained in F. S. Regs., Part II. and the Staff Manual respectively. Title pages will be prepared in manuscript.

Place	Date	Hour	Summary of Events and Information	Remarks and references to Appendices
In the Field	Feb. 1918			
	1		Lt. J. ALMOND arrives from Aerial Observation Course.	2.99
	2		Lt. F.T. BLENNERHASSET returns from Course of Mined dug-out construction.	2.99
	3		Major J. NALL assumes command at H.Q. vice Lt. Col INCHES to Senior Officers' Course in U.K.	2.99
	5		Lt. A.E. BIRTWISTLE arrives from leave in U.K. and Lt. A.C. SANDYS proceeded to leave to U.K.	2.99
			2/Lt. K. MACIVER transferred to U.K. sick, and struck off the strength of the Bde.	
	7		Major D. BROWN returned from B.C's Course in U.K.	2.99
			2/Lt. J.A. LECHERTIER C.211 attached to D.211.	
			Military Medals announced for 710194 Sgt. W. Halliwell and 710356 Gnr. S Hardcastle.	
			Belgian CROIX DE GUERRE awarded to Lt. H.W.L. KEARNS A.211, 31906 B.S.M. J.H. Nicholls,	
			710302 Dvr. S. Cunliffe, and 710356 Gnr. S. Hardcastle.	
	9		2/Lt. J.R. RHODES admitted to hospital sick.	2.99
	14		211th. Bde supported raid by 9th. Batt. Manchesters on MACKENSEN TRENCH 7 prisoners and	2.99
			1 machine gun captured.	
	15		Lt. G.H. DREWRY returned from leave in U.K.	2.99
			Week's campaign in war savings campaign £1199.7.6.	
			Half of each Battery relieved by half Batteries of 55th. D.A.	
			Lt. J.J. COWIESON proceeded on 14 days' leave to U.K. and Capt. J. WADDELL A.V.C. returned.	
	16		Remainder of Batteries relieved by remainder of 55th. D.A.	2.99
			G.O.C. complimented B.211 on excellence of their turn-out	
			Capt. J.F. WARD proceeded on 14 days' leave to U.K. Lt. F.B. LONG 1/3 Fd. Amb. attached for duty.	
			Capt. Rev. A.C. TRENCH transferred to H.Q. Canadian Corps.	
	18		Training programme put into operation. (211th. Bde . having moved into G.H.Q. reserve – A. and B.	2.99
			Batteries at VENDIN-LES-BETHUNE, C. and D. and Bde . H.Q. at AMMEZIN.) 16th.	
			Signalling refresher course instituted at Bde H.Q.	
	19		Elementary training carried on.	2.99
	21		G.O.C. 127th. Inf. Bde. consulted with reference to joint tactical training with the Infantry.	2.99
	22		Two Lewis guns per Battery issued, authorised	2.99
			Lt. A.C. SANDYS arrived from 14 days' leave in U.K.	
	25		Lt. E.E. CANDLISH proceeded on 14 days' leave to U.K.	2.99
	26		Tactical reconnaissance of LOCON area.	2.99
	27		Second week's training begun. Individual training.	2.99
	28		Tactical reconnaissance of 11th. Div. area from LOOS to LA BASSEE CANAL.	2.99
			Lectures to N.C.Os by Div. Commander. Lt. Col E.J. INCHES returned from Sen. Os' Course.	
			Lt. F.H. ROWE attached O.i/c signal sub section vice Lt. J.B. TOMMIS to Div. Signals.	

42nd Divisional Artillery.

211th BRIGADE

ROYAL FIELD ARTILLERY

MARCH 1 9 1 8

Vol 14

Confidential

211 Bde RFA.
WAR DIARY
MARCH 1918.
From 1/3/18 To 31/3/18
Volume 15.

211th Bde. R.F.A.　　MARCH 1918.

3rd	211 Bde moved from ANNEZIN to AMES near LILLERS.	
	Lt J.J. COWIESON A.211 rejoins from leave in U.K. Capt. L.D. MACK HQ.211 proceeded on 14 days' leave to U.K.	3.9.9
4th–17th	Mobile training by Batteries.	
4th	Lieut A.E. BIRTWISTLE C.211 attached to HQ.211. Major V. KILVERT C.211 rejoins from B.C's Course, SHOEBURYNESS.	5.9.9
5th	Lieut D.F. MACKENZIE A.211 and 2/Lieut T.KNOWLES D.211, proceeded on 14 days' leave to U.K.	3.9.9
7th	Lieut E. FORTH B.211 rejoins from 1st Army Artillery School.	8.9.9
9th	2/Lieut M.G. WELLS B.211 rejoins from hospital.	8.9.9
12th	2/Lieut A.B. DYKE B.211 and 2/Lieut A.W.J. TALBOT A.211 proceeded on 14 days' leave to U.K.	8.9.9
13th	Lieut (A/Capt) G.A.S. COLLIN C.211 promoted Captain with effect from 13.1.'18. (Auth'y. London Gazette 18.1.'19)	8.9.9
14th	2/Lieut J.R. RHODES D.211 rejoins from hospital. Capt. G.A.S. COLLIN C.211 proceeded on 7 days' leave to PARIS.	1.9.9
15th	Capt. M.F. THOMPSON D.211 to B.C's Course SHOEBURYNESS.	8.9.9
18th	Calibration Range used by 18 pdr Batteries.	6.9.9
19th	Capt. L.D. MACK HQ.211 rejoins from leave in U.K.	8.9.9
20th	Calibration Range used by 18 pdr Batteries.	8.9.9
	Calibration by 4.5" How. on Army Calibration Range.	8.2.9
23rd	Major V. KILVERT C.211 proceeded on Gas Course at CHOQUES.	7.9.9
	211 Bde dumped surplus kit on marched at 3 hours notice to CAUCOURT – 6 miles S. of BRUAY. Capt G.A.S. COLLIN C.211 rejoins from leave in PARIS.	8.9.9
	2/Lieut J.R. RHODES D.211 posted to 42 DAC.	
	2/Lieut A.W.J. TALBOT A.211 to hospital while on leave in U.K.	
24th	Major V. KILVERT C.211 rejoins from Gas Course. Lieut A.E. BIRTWISTLE C.211 attachment to M.G. 211 ceases.	
	211 Bde marched South for BAVINCOURT – orders received en route for Brigade to march through to ADINFER.	
	(8 miles S. of ARRAS) where the Bde bivouaced.	
	Lieut D.F. MACKENZIE A.211 rejoins from leave in U.K.	2.9.9
25th 1 a.m	Word received that the Enemy had broken through and was marching on GOMIECOURT – the 211th Bde proceeded at once to valley behind COURCELLES where the Batteries came into action before dawn – 42nd Division holding the line reinforced by 42 Division with 1 Bde 31st Division supporting the left flank.	2.9.9
noon	Word received that the Enemy had broken through at BABAUME and were advancing on BIHUCOURT – 211 Bde opened fire at extreme range to place barrage East of BIHUCOURT and then advanced to G.2 and G.8. S. of LOGEAST WOOD.	2.9.9
6 p.m.	211 Bde withdrew to former position behind COURCELLES.	2.9.9
11 p.m	211 Bde withdrew to position in F.29 S. of ABLAINZEVILLE in order to cover 42nd INF. who had fallen back on COURCELLES – LOGEAST WOOD line.	2.9.9
	Lieut M.W.L. KEARNS A.211 attachment to N.Q.42 D.A. ceases.	

WAR DIARY (Sheet 2)
INTELLIGENCE SUMMARY
(Erase heading not required.)

Army Form C. 2118.

MAY 1918

Place	Date	Hour	Summary of Events and Information	Remarks and references to Appendices
	26th	8 a.m.	2 Sections per Batty. withdrew to positions S.E of ESSARTS in F.19.	E.J.J.
		9 a.m.	Remaining sections withdrew after main body of Infantry had fallen back to ABLAINZEVILLE – BUCQUOY Line.	E.J.J.
		2.55 p.m.	Barrage put down by Right Group: (2/10th Btn. under Lt.Col. INCHES) an enemy were reported advancing. Long columns of Enemy Entering ACHIET-LE-PETIT shelled by Right Group. Liaison officers kept with Battn. HQrs and communicated by runner, until visual was established in afternoon 26th.	E.J.J.
	27th	6.55 a.m.	S.O.S. received by phone. Barrage put down up to 9.40 a.m.	E.J.J.
		noon	Heavy enemy barrage on front line. M.G and rifle fire heard ∞ S.O.S. barrage put down by Right Group.	E.J.J.
		1.35 p.m.	Message from Yorks Regt (on immediate right of 127 INF Bde.) timed 1.35 p.m. states enemy to have attacked BUCQUOY soon after noon in 3 waves – first wave driven back by M.G and rifle fire, second and third waves caught in Artillery barrage.	E.J.J.
		11 a.m.– 2.30 p.m.	Right Group Battery positions heavily shelled by enemy.	E.J.J.
		2 p.m.	Enemy reported by 1/7 Manchesters to be massing in ABLAINZEVILLE – Engaged by Right Group. (Reported later by prisoner to have annihilated one Battalion).	E.J.J.
		4 p.m.	Message 5 p.m. intercepted from VISUAL Station saying enemy attacking BUCQUOY. and again 5 p.m. Barrage put down for short period – No confirmation of attack received.	E.J.J.
		6.30 p.m.	Liaison officer reports line intact. Throughout the day telephone communication held – or if broken was instantly repaired – between Battn. HQrs and Right Group Headquarters. Visual station established 26th inst just W of BUCQUOY in bivouac communication with Battn. forward and Right Group in rear. No communication with Division Hqrs. except by D.R.L.S.	E.J.J.
			Early morning 27th 127 INF Bde. HQrs moved into close proximity of Right Group Hqrs, so that Right Group Liaison officer withdrawn from INF Bde, their officers remain in Liaison at Battn. Hqrs.	E.J.J.
	28th	9.5 a.m.	Heavy gun & M.G fire S. East of BUCQUOY.	E.J.J.
		9.30 a.m.	Bombardment by enemy of front and support lines BUCQUOY	E.J.J.
		9.35 a.m.	127 INF Bde. report Low flying E.A very troublesome.	E.J.J.
		9.45 a.m.	Heavy barrage in BUCQUOY road.	E.J.J.

Army Form C. 2118.

WAR DIARY (Sheet 3)
or
INTELLIGENCE SUMMARY.
(Erase heading not required.)

MAR 1918

Instructions regarding War Diaries and Intelligence Summaries are contained in F. S. Regs., Part II. and the Staff Manual respectively. Title pages will be prepared in manuscript.

Place	Date	Hour	Summary of Events and Information	Remarks and references to Appendices
	28th	9.55am	Slow fire opened in Counter Preparation by Right Group.	F.J.9
		10.50"	Fire by both sides died down.	
		11.40"	Message received from 126th INF Bde (on left of 127th INF Bde) that enemy had been driven back on their front – W & N of ABLAINZEVILLE.	
		10.20"	Telephone and visual communication with Battn. temporarily destroyed.	F.J.9
		11.45"	Message from liaison officer that enemy attacked 10.50am but was met in the open.	F.J.9
		1.32pm	Barrage put down by Left Hand Batterie B.2.11 & C.2.11 on liaison officers reported bombing raid by enemy.	F.J.9
		2.50"	Situation quieter – 4.5" Hows. fired on NISSEN HUTS S. of ABLAINZEVILLE in F.30 & 59 D.A. assisting. Hubs reported full of enemy – liaison officer ranges the Batteries.	W.J.9
			During 28th inst. the weather broke and rain coming down all afternoon.	
	Night 28/29th		Harassing fire during night maintained by Right Group. 8-18pdrs and 2-4.5" Hows. of 293 Bde came into action behind ESSARTS under R. Group.	F.J.9
			2/Lieut M.G. WELLS B.2.11 killed – shell 28th.	F.J.9
	29th		Quiet day – weather again good.	
		Dusk	9 more 18pdrs of 293 AFA Bde came into action (making 3-18pdr Batteries and 1 section of 4.5" Hows. Batty. for 293 Bde).	F.J.9
		8.25am	Enemy reported massing in LOGEAST WOOD – guns opened for 20 mins.	F.J.9
	Night 29/30		41st Division relieved 42nd Division (Zero Arty.) in BUCQUOY sector.	F.J.9
	30th		Quiet day – Harassing fire day and night by Rt. Group – weather unsettled towards evening.	F.J.9
	31st	7.35pm	2 mins. concentration of fire by enemy on BUCQUOY.	F.J.9
		7.5am	Enemy bombardment on DERVILLE FARM – AYETTE road.	F.J.9
		4.15 "	Counter preparation fire by Right Group.	F.J.9
		7.30 "	Guns of both sides died down.	F.J.9
		5 pm	Weather broke again – heavy rain during night – situation unchanged.	F.J.9

SUMMARY.

	O.	O.R.		O.	O.R.
Casualties Killed	1	11	From Courses	2	39
" wounded	–	37	" Hospital	1	15
From Leave	5	19	" Postings to Bde.	–	35
			" from "	1	3

	O.	O.R.
On leave	2	51
" Courses	2	12
" Hospital	1	25

E. C. Irvine Lieut-Colonel.
Commanding 2.11 Bde R.F.A.

42nd Div.
IV.Corps.

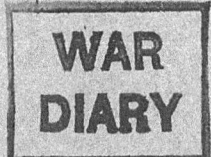

Headquarters,

211th BRIGADE, R.F.A.

A P R I L

1 9 1 8

CONFIDENTIAL

War Diary
of
211th. Brigade R.F.A.

from 1st. April 1918 to 30th. April 1918.

Volume 16.

WAR DIARY
or
INTELLIGENCE SUMMARY.
(Erase heading not required.)

Instructions regarding War Diaries and Intelligence Summaries are contained in F. S. Regs., Part II. and the Staff Manual respectively. Title pages will be prepared in manuscript.

Place	Date 1918 FEB APR	Hour	Summary of Events and Information	Remarks and references to Appendices
In the Field.	1st.		42nd. Div. Infantry relieved 41st. Div. Infantry in BUCQUOY Sector. D.211. heavily shelled - 2 HOWS. destroyed, 4 HOWS. sent to Workshops.	
"	2nd.		Front and support trenches shelled (BUCQUOY) by 5.9" HOW. and 77 mm. gun. Enemy working during night 2/3rd. on crest 100 yds. E of our line. Lieut. E.Forth B.211 Transferred to England - sick -	
"	3rd.		During night 2/3rd. 32nd. Division on our left successfully attacked AYETTE. zero hour 2 a m Weather unsettled.	
"	"		Capt. C.I.Scowcroft A.211 Rejoins from B.C's Course SHOEBURYNESS. D.211	
"	4th.		M.F.Thompson Right Group bring up extra ammunition and register points near ROSSIGNOL WOOD on front of 3/5th. Div. (On our right.)	
"	5th.	5 am to 10 a.m.	Harassing fire kept up night and day by Right Group. Heavy gas and H.E. bombardment of support line, ESSARTS and vally north and south of ESSARTS by enemy (continuous rain night 4/5th. - no wind)	
"	"	10.5 a.m.	Enemy Infantry attack centre of 42nd. Div. front in BUCQUOY. All Lewis guns and rifles clogged with mud, all telephones communication broken, visual impossible owing to mist. runners difficult to get through surrounding gas. Slow barrage put down by Right Group 10.20am in response to message by runner from Group O.P.	
"	"		1/5th. Fusiliers forced back 500 yards in centre, 1/5th. Fusiliers on right flank fell back north of BUCQUOY to conform.	
"	"	5.30 a.m.	3/5th. Division attacked ROSSIGNOL WOOD supported by 4-18pdr. Btys. and 1-4.5" How. Bty. of Right Group. 42nd. D.A. - second objective captured - Rain all day.	
"	6th.		Sky clear - ground drying - Harassing fire kept up by Right Group. Positions for 3 Brigades of Right Group reconnoitred W. of FONQUEVILLERS to cover Purple line. Evening of 6th. 293rd. A.F.A. Bde. withdrawn from Right Group. Lieut. J.R. Tommis (42nd. Div. Sig. Coy.) att.Hqrs. To C.C.S - gunshot wound -	
"	7th.	7.30 a.m.	S.O.S. on Right Battn. front received by phone - Enemy skirmishers advanced towards centre of BUCQUOY, but 3 waves waiting in hollows E. of village were caught in Artillery barrage - No strong attack developed.	
"	"		Morning clear - midday slight rain. - Evening of 7th. A/26 A.F.A. Bde. came into action under Right Group.- D.211 return into action with 4-4.5" HOWS. (Throughout April as in last 10 days of March E.A. and E.O.B. were very troublesome.)	
"	8th.	4 am	Lieut. F.H.Potter (42nd. Div. Sig. Coy.) attached to Bde. Hqrs. Gas and H.E. bombardment by enemy of ESSARTS area - C.295 came into action under Right Group.	
"	"	5 am	Counter Preparation put down by Right Group.- Enemy fire died down.	

WAR DIARY
or
INTELLIGENCE SUMMARY.

(Erase heading not required.)

Instructions regarding War Diaries and Intelligence Summaries are contained in F. S. Regs., Part II. and the Staff Manual respectively. Title pages will be prepared in manuscript.

Place	Date 1918 FEB APR	Hour	Summary of Events and Information	Remarks and references to Appendices
In the Field	8th.		Rain all day – 62nd. Div. less Artillery relieve 42nd. Div. less Artillery.	
"	9th.		Weather dull but fine – very heavy underfoot.	
"	"	7 am	Enemy shelled support line with occasional bursts on front line.	
"	10th.	9 am	Enemy shelling continues.– Counter Preparation put down by Right Group.	
"	"		Quiet day – Rain towards evening – 116th. Battery relieved C.295 (Personnel changed, guns handed over) in Right Group.– Command of Artillery covering 62nd. Div. passes to C.R.A.	
"	"	11 a.m.	62nd. Div. 11 a.m.	
"	11th.		Capt. J. Waddell (A.V.C) att. B.211 – To 431 Coy. A.S.C.	
"	"		312th. Bde. comes under Right Group – A/26 and 116th. Battery rejoin Left Group.	
"	"		Right Group Hqrs. move near INF. Bde. F.23.d.3.3. – Lieut-Col. MASON takes over Command	
"	"		Right Group with 211th. Hqrs. Staff. – Lieut-Col. INCHES goes to wagon line for rest.	
"	"		Lieut. G.H.DREWRY Hqrs. – To Hospital – sick –	
"	12th.		Capt. M.F.THOMPSON D.211 To Hospital – sick –	
"	13th.		Group Hqrs. moves to F.23.c.7.6	
"	14th.		Capt. F.C.HOWARD (R.A.M.C) attached to A.211.	
"	15th.		Lieut. G.HIREWRY Hqrs. transferred to England.	
"	16th.		B.Cs 210th. and 211th. Bde. reconnoit re positions of 310th. and 187th. Bdes.	
"	"		2/Lieut. V.R.CLARKE B.211 Posted from 1/42nd. D.A.C.	
"	17th.		J.P.HEYWORTH B.211 – Wounded – shell –	
"	18th.		Personnel A.B. and C.211 exchange guns and positions with A.B. and C.187th Bde.and 211th.	
"	"		Bde. comes under C.R.A., 42nd. Div. and forms part of Left Group under Col. CARDEW 190th. Bde.	
"	"		Lieut. A.E.BIRTWISTLE C.211. attached to Bde. Hqrs.	
"	19th.		125th. INF. Bde. raided M.G. post K.11.b. under box barrage in which 211th. Bde. formed part.	
"	"		28 casualties to horses in forward wagon lines at BIENVILLERS.	
"	20th.		Forward wagon lines rejoin rear W.L. at SOUASTRE.	
"	"		One section B.211 moved into action E. of FONQUEVILLERS E.22.a.	
"	21st.		Remainder B.211 move into action E.22.a.4.5.	
"	22nd.		One section A.211 " " " " E.22.c.	
"	23rd.		Remainder A.211 " " " " "	
"	24th.		Lieut. F.J.G.JACKSON C.211 Posted to C.210th.Bde. to be 2nd. in Command.	
"	26th.		One section D.211 move into action E.22.d.	
"	27th.		Remainder D.211 " " " " "	
"	"		Two Hows. placed forward in E.28.b.	

WAR DIARY
or
INTELLIGENCE SUMMARY.
(Erase heading not required.)

Instructions regarding War Diaries and Intelligence Summaries are contained in F. S. Regs., Part II. and the Staff Manual respectively. Title pages will be prepared in manuscript.

Place	Date 1918	Hour	Summary of Events and Information	Remarks and references to Appendices
In the Field	28th.	A.M.	One forward How. damaged withdrawn to W.L. Remaining forward How. rejoined main gun position.	2,9
	29th.		Lieut. J.J.COWIESON A.211 attached to 42nd. D.A.C.	
	30th.		Damaged How. repaired and brought into action in forward position in E.29.d (10th. 211th & 187th Bdes.) 187th. Bde. relieve 190th. Bde. and assume control of left group (10th. 211th & 187th Bdes.) Lieut-Colonel.INGLES returns from W.L. to Battle Hqrs. and assumes Command of 20th & 211th Bdes.	2,9

SUMMARY

	O.	O.R.		O.	O.R.
Casualties - Killed	-	4	Postings to Bde.	1	134
-Wounded	2	63	" from "	-	6
From leave.	-	46	On Courses	-	2
" Courses	-	10	To Hosp'l.	2	93
" Hospital	-	20			

F. J. Ingles.
Lieut-Colonel,
Commanding, 211th. Brigade R.F.A.

C O N F I D E N T I A L.

War Diary
of
211th. Brigade R.F.A.

From 1st. May 1918 to 31st. May 1918.

Volume 117.

Army Form C. 2118.

WAR DIARY
or
INTELLIGENCE SUMMARY.
(Erase heading not required.)

Instructions regarding War Diaries and Intelligence Summaries are contained in F.S. Regs., Part II. and the Staff Manual respectively. Title pages will be prepared in manuscript.

Place	Date	Hour	Summary of Events and Information	Remarks and references to Appendices
Field.	1917 MAY 2nd.		2/Lieut. SHERRY J.A. C.211 Posted from 42nd. D.A.C. Lieut. COWIESON J.J. A.211 Posted to 42nd. D.A.C.	
	4th.		During afternoon A.211 & B.211 fired THERMIT into ROSSIGNOL WOOD. 211th. Bde. assisted in box barrage on ROSSIGNOL WOOD whilst 1st. New Zealand INF. Bde. attacked on right flank. Major HIGHTON L. D.211 Wounded - Gunshot. - Lieut. OSMASTON G.H. att. Hqrs. Signal officer from 42nd. Div. Sig. Coy. - Lieut. POTTER F.H. att Hqrs. to 4th. Corps Sigs.	
	5th.		Lieut-Col. E.J.INCHES. assumes command of left group (210th. & 211th F.A. Bdes.) at 9 p.m. Lieut. KEARNS H.W.L. A.211 Posted as 2nd. in Command to D.211. Lieut. BEARD H.E. C.211 Posted from 42nd. D.A.C.	
	6th.		42nd. Division less Artillery relieved in Left Sector IV Corps by 57th. Division less Artillery. — Command of Artillery (210th. & 211th.Bdes. Left group) covering 57.th Division	
	7th.		Passes to C.R.A. 41st. Division.	
	8th.		Capt. COLLIN G.A.S C.211 Posted to Command D.211. - Capt. JACKSON F.J.G. C.211 Posted from 210th. Bde.	
	10th.		2/Lieut. GRANT J.K. C.211 To Hospital — sick —	
	11th.		C.211 (Silent Battery) shelled heavily by 8" Armour Piercing - 6" How. Battery close to C.211 had previously carried out destructive shoot on enemy battery - C.211 had been silent since 19.4.18. - Gas bombardment of FONQUEVILLERS mainly Yellow Cross, 7 p.m. to 8.40 p.m.	
	12th.		Command of Artillery covering 57th. Division passes to C.R.A. 57th. Division.- Silent hours inaugurated, during which no battery fires — object, to assist sound-rangers. A/Major CULLIN G.A.S. D.211 Posted to C.211 to be 2nd. in Command. - Capt. JACKSON F.J.G. C.211 Posted to 210th. Bde. - A/Capt. KEARNS H.W.L. D.211 Posted to A.211, relinquishes acting rank. - A/Major FORSYTH A.F.J. D.211 Posted from A/174th. Bde. R.F.A. - Capt. BROWN C.R. A.211 Posted from 210th. Bde. - Capt. SCOWCROFT C.I. A.211 Posted to 210th Bde. Capt. THOMPSON M.F. D.211 Posted from Base. Batteries reconnoitre position to cover rear system known as the RED LINE.	
	13th.		Weather breaks — rain all day.	
	14th.		weather fine, warm dry — Gas-concentration put down by D.210, D.211 in conjunction with H.A. Lieut. MALCOLM D. att.A.211 From R.A.H.Q.	
	15th.		Dry, fine warm. - Lieut. KEARNS H.W.L. A.211 Attached to R.A.H.Q.	
	16th.		Dry, fine warm. - 62nd. Division less Artillery relieve 37th. Division less Artillery on immediate left of 57th.Division.- 37th.Division move into Corps reserve.	
	17th.		Dry. fine warm.— O.ps and visual stations for Red Line reconnoitred.	

Army Form C. 2118.

WAR DIARY
or
INTELLIGENCE SUMMARY.
(Erase heading not required.)

Instructions regarding War Diaries and Intelligence Summaries are contained in F. S. Regs., Part II. and the Staff Manual respectively. Title pages will be prepared in manuscript.

Place	Date 1918 May	Hour	Summary of Events and Information	Remarks and references to Appendices
Field.	18th		Dry, fine warm.- Positions reconnoitred to cover Chateau de la Hale/Switch line, an intermediate line between Purple and Red lines.	2.9.9.
	19th.		Dry, fine warm.	2.9.9.
	20th.		Dry, fine warm.- Lieut-Col. MASON takes over command of Left Group.- In the evening 170th. INF. Bde. raided post K.12 for identification - Artillery support by 211th. Bde reported satisfactory.	2.9.9.
	21st.		Dry, fine warm.- 170th. INF. Bde. raid post L.7.c. - with Artillery support by 210th. and 211th. Bdes.- Post found unoccupied.	2.9.9.
	22nd.		Dry, fine warm.- 170th. INF. Bde. attempted raid without Artillery support - raiders stopped by hostile fire before leaving our trenches.	2.9.9.
	23rd.		Clouds - dull. 170th. INF. Bde. raid hostile post L.7.c. with support from 4.5" Hows. Artillery support reported excellent by Battalion Commander.- Post unoccupied. Lieut. SANDYS A.C. D.211 To Anti-Gas Course.	2.9.9.
	24th.		Rain all day.	
	25th.		Lieut. GARDINER R.W. Hqrs. Posted from 59th. Battery, 18th. Army Bde. R.F.A. Fine.- 171st. Bde.(on right) use one Company as raiding party against enemy posts K.11.- Artillery support by Right Group to whom 210th.& 211th. Bdes. are lent to assist in operation.- 13 prisoners secured.	2.9.9.
	26th.		Lieut. STEPHENSON G. B.211 Posted from D.A.C. Clouds.- warm.	2.9.9.
	27th.		Gas bombardment of FONQUEVILLERS area 2.15 a.m. to 3.15 a.m.- 171st. Bde. raided ROSSIGNOL WOOD at 6.15 p.m.- B.211 lent to Right Group to support.- Dry, fine warm.	2.9.9.
	28th.		2/Lieut. TINDELL J.W. A.211 Posted from 42nd. D.A.C. Fine - warm.	2.9.9.
	29th.		Capt. (Rev) MYERSCOUGH J. B.211 attached from 42nd. D.A.	2.9.9.

SUMMARY.

	O.	OR.		O.	OR.
Casualties					
Killed		3	From Hospital		8
wounded	1	21	" Courses		5
From leave	2	2	Postings to Bde.	8	220
			" from "	2	16
			On Courses	1	9
			To Hospl.	1	83
			On leave		4

Vol 17

CONFIDENTIAL

War Diary
of
211th. Brigade R.F.A.
from 1st June 1918 to 30th. June 1918.

Volume 18.

Army Form C. 2118.

WAR DIARY
or
INTELLIGENCE SUMMARY.
(Erase heading not required.)

Instructions regarding War Diaries and Intelligence Summaries are contained in F. S. Regs., Part II. and the Staff Manual respectively. Title pages will be prepared in manuscript.

Place	Date 1917	Hour	Summary of Events and Information	Remarks and references to Appendices
Field	1st	3.30 am	Fire false S.O.S. B.211 one gun damaged.	
	2nd		Major J. Nall Awarded D.S.O. Fire Gas bombardment of battery area round FONQUEVILLERS. Raid by 170th Inf. Bde. postponed. Lieut A.C. Sandys rejoins from Gas Course	
	3rd		Bright, warm. B.211 move 2 guns.	
	4th		Raid by 170 Inf. Bde on trench in L.7.c. failed. — 42nd. Division relieve N.Z. Div on our right. Lieut.D.Malcolm att A.211 Rejoins R.A.H.Q.	
	5th		Fine and warm. D.211 moved 2 guns to E.23.d.	
	6th		Fine and hot.	
	7th		Major J. Nall A.211 and Major D. Brown B.211 mentioned in despatches.	
	9th		Lieut-Col INCHES takes over Command Left Group (210th & 211th Bdes) Lieut-Col MASON goes to wagon line SOUASTRE. Evening 9th. D.211 withdraw 2 hows. back to main position E.22.a., the detached position in E.23.d. having been constantly shelled. — some rain - dull.	
	10th		Warm — fine. 2/Lieut J.A.Lechertier D.211 and Lieut A.C.Sandys D.211 to Hospital — sick. " J.A.Crom to U.K on 14 days leave.	
	13th.		Evening 13/14th one section B.210 moves from E.22.d. to F.13.d. near ESSARTS. Lieut.G.Stephenson B.211 Attached to N.Z.Div T.Ms	
	14th		2/Lieut J.A. Sherry C.211 —do— Night 14th/15th 172nd. INF. Bde relieved in Left Sector by 171st INF Bde. Warm — fine 2/Lieut W.N.Cryer A.211 To Veterinery Course.	
	15th to 20th		Fine and warm. Registration by balloon carried out.	
	15th		Lieut R.M.Garnett A.211 Wounded — shell	
	16th		Lieut.E.N.James att D.211 From C.210 Bde R"T"A.	
	17th		Capt. Williams att B.211 From 9th' Kings Liverpool Regt.	
	20th.		Rain - Projected raid by 2/6th Battn. Kings, Liverpool on dug outs in K.11.c postponed	
	21st.		Raid carried out under Artillery support Left Group under Lieut-Col MASON constituted for raid as follows. — 210th., 211th., C/286th and 11th & 12th N.Z Batteries Barrage reported by INFANTRY to be excellent. — 1 Prisoner and 1 M.G. captured. Prisoner reports barrage to be accurate. Diversion carried out during raid by A 211 with co-operation by 6" Hows.	

Army Form C. 2118.

WAR DIARY
or
INTELLIGENCE SUMMARY.
(Erase heading not required.)

Place	Date	Hour	Summary of Events and Information	Remarks and references to Appendices
Field	1919 Jan 23rd		2/Lieut V.R. Clarke B.211 To 3rd. Army Rest Camp	
	24th		" J.A. Bechertier D.211 Rejoins from Hospital	
	26th		" W.N. Cryer A.211 Rejoins from Veterinary Course.	
			Lieut. J.Harland att B.211 From D.A.C.	
			Capt. Williams att B.211 Rejoins 9th. Kings Liverpool Regt.	

SUMMARY

	O.	O.R		O.	O.R.
Casualties Killed			Postings to Bde.		84
" Wounded	1	4	" from	1	30
" Hospital	1	9	On Courses	1	10
From leave	1	13	To Hospital	2	86
" Courses	2	6	On leave	2	18

Vol 18

CONFIDENTIAL.

WAR DIARY
of
211th Brigade R.F.A.
From 1st July 1918 to 31st July 1918.
VOLUME 19.

WAR DIARY
INTELLIGENCE SUMMARY
(Erase heading not required.)

Army Form C. 2118.

Place	1918 Date	Hour	Summary of Events and Information	Remarks and references to Appendices
Field	Jul 1		Captain R.W. Gardiner H.Q. London Gazette 1.6.18 Promoted Capt. with precedence 1.6.16.	
	4		Lieut. G. Stephenson B.211 rejoins from N.Z. D.f Ms. 2/Lieut. J.A.Croll D.211 rejoins from leave in U.K. 2/Lieut. J.K. Grant C.211 struck off strength with effect from 10.5.18. Authority 42nd Division No. 222/457 dated 2.7.18.	
	5		1section per battery exchanged guns in situ with 3rd N.Z. F.A. Bde found SAILLY-AU-BOIS. Remainder of 211th Bde. exchanged guns in situ with 3rd N.Z.F.A. Bde. 211th Bde became Left Group 42nd D.A. with Headquarters at SAILLY covering 126 INF. Bde.	
	7		2/Lieut J.A. Sherry C.211 Posted to 42nd Div. T.Ms.	
	8		Lieut. Harland T. attd. B.211 rejoins D.A.C. Lieut. A.E. Birtwistle C.211 to hospital sick.	
	13		D.211 destroyed light railway K.34.	
			2/Lieut.W.M. Shelley B.211 granted 14 days' leave to U.K. 2/Lieut. V. Clarke B.211 rejoins from Third Army Rest Camp.	
	15		211th Bde. fired barrage in support of N.Z. Division on left minor operation.	
			2/Lieut. J.A. Lemartier D.211 granted 14 days' leave to U.K. Lieut A.E. Birtwistle C.211 rejoins from hospital. 2/Lieut. P.W. Stevens A.211 to Officers' Rest House PARIS PLAGE.	
	16 11.30 a.m.		211th Bde. bombarded trenches K.23 in conjunction with N.A. smelling of PUISIEUX. During the day 211th Bde disperse enemy deploying for attack against 17th T.S. Coy.	
	17		D.211 carry out registration in conjunction with 17th F.S. Coy.	
	18		2/Lieut. A.J. Rogerson A.211 posted from D.A.C. 2/Lieut. A Young C.211 posted from D.A.C.	
	19		127 INF. Bde. established advanced posts in K.22 and K.28 with assistance from 4.5 Hows.	
	20		2/Lieut. W.N. Cryer A.211 to U.K. on 14 days' leave.	
			211th Bde. 18 Pdrs fired barrage in support of raid by 63rd R.N. Divn. (on right)	
	21		Lieut. E.M. Fry D.211 posted from D.A.C.	
			Captain L.D. Mack H.Q. granted 10 days' leave in France (Paris)	
			Major Hall J, D.S.O. A.211 attd. Bde. H.Q.	
	22		2/Lieut. P.W. Stevens A.211 from Rest House Paris Plage.	
	23		Lieut. Colonel E.J. INGHES, D.S.O. H.Q. to U.K. on 14 days' special leave.	
			Lieut. D.F. Mackenzie A.211 Posted to 42nd D.A.C. Lieut. A.C. Sandys D.211 from hospital	
			211th Bde. fired barrage in support of operation by 125 INF. Bde. N.Z. INF established through K.22.J. and K.23.C.	
	24		Captain F. Knowles B.211 granted 10 days' leave in France. Lieut H.W. James D.211 Posted from C.210 F.A. Bde. Lieut. H.E. Beard C.211 attached to A.211. Lieut. A.C. Sandys D.211 attached to B.211.	
	26		Lieut. J. Almond B.211 to U.K. on 14 days' leave.	

Army Form C. 2118.

WAR DIARY

INTELLIGENCE SUMMARY.

(Erase heading not required.)

Instructions regarding War Diaries and Intelligence Summaries are contained in F. S. Regs., Part II. and the Staff Manual respectively. Title pages will be prepared in manuscript.

Place	Date	Hour	Summary of Events and Information	Remarks and references to Appendices
Field	1918 28		1/7 Manchester Rgt. Operation to capture and consolidate CETORIX. Group prepared to fire protective barrage - barrage not required. FRONT LINE readjusted CETORIX - JEAN HART - JENA TRENCH - PUB STREET	
	29th		2/Lieut. W.H. Shelley B.211 rejoins from leave in U.K. Lieut. E.N. James D.211 granted 14 days' leave in U.K. 2/Lieut. F.T. Hammerhassett C.211 from leave in U.K. leave extended 26.7.18 Authority Medical Certificate War Office.	
	30th		V Corps carried out feint attack by means of smoke barrage and artillery bombardment - Left Group fired smoke barrage in support and bombarded trench system in K.34.d.	
	31		2/Lieut. B.A. Blackborow C.211 to U.K. on 14 days' leave.
2/Lieut. J.A. Lechertier D.211 from leave in France.
Captain F. Knowles B.211 from leave in U.K.	

SUMMARY.

	Officers	O.R.		Officers	O.R.
Casualties Wounded	-	3	Postings to Bn.	4	53.
From leave	5	30	from Bn.	2	9
From Hospital	2	48	On Courses	1	31
From Courses	1	15	To Hospital	19	144
			On Leave.		73.

CONFIDENTIAL.

WAR DIARY
of
211th Brigade, R.F.A.

from 1st August 1918 to 31st August, 1918.

VOLUME 20.

Army Form C. 2118.

WAR DIARY
or
INTELLIGENCE SUMMARY.
(Erase heading not required.)

Instructions regarding War Diaries and Intelligence Summaries are contained in F. S. Regs., Part II. and the Staff Manual respectively. Title pages will be prepared in manuscript.

Place	Date	Hour	Summary of Events and Information	Remarks and references to Appendices
Field.	1918 Aug 2nd		Captain L.D. Mack H.Q. from leave in France. Lieut. A.E. Birtwistle 'C' to Third Army Arty. school. Major D. Brown 'B' proceeded on leave to Paris.	
	4th.		211th Bde. bombarded advanced enemy trenches S of LA SIGNY FARM in support of a minor operation by 126th INF Bde.	
			Lieut. E.N. JAMES 'D' admitted to hospital sick in U.K. Lieut., H.E. BEARD 'C' posted to 'A'	
	5th.		2/Lieut. J.A. LECHERTIER 'D' posted to 'A'.	
	7th.		2/Lieut. W.N. CRYER 'A' from leave in U.K. Lieut. A.C. SANDYS attd" B"211 rejoins 'D'	
	10th.		Lieut. J. ALMOND 'A' from leave in U.K.	
	11th.		2/Lieut. H. TOPPING 'D' proceeded to U.K. on 14 days" leave. Capt. R.W. GARDINER 'H.Q.' attd. 'A'. 2/Lieut. J.A. LECHERTIER 'A' attd. H.Q.	
	14th		Fine, dry warm. 'B' and 'C' Btys and 1 Sec. 'D' moved forward to positions W of LA SIGNY FARM consequent on withdrawal by the enemy from the SERRE salient.	
			Major D. BROWN from leave in France. 2/Lieut. B.A. BLACKBOROW 'C' from leave in U.K. Weather threatening	
	15th		'A' and 'C' Btys and remainder 'D' moved forward W of LA SIGNY FARM.	
			but fine. Heavy shelling of batteries during the day.	
	16th		'A' sidestepped 500 yds. Owing to persistent hostile shelling. Routes to SERRE reconnoitred.	
			Enemy on line BUCQUOY - PUISIEUX - BEAUCOURT.	
	17th		2/Lieut. F.T. BLENNERHASSETT 'C' attd. 'H.Q.'. 2/Lieut. J.A. LECHERTIER attd. 'H.Q.' rejoins 'A'. 2/Lieut. F.W. STEVENS 'A' proceeded to U.K. on 14 days" leave.	
	19th		Lieut. H.E. BEARD 'A' to Third Army Artillery School. Lieut. G.H. STEPHENSON 'B' attd. 'C' Weather fine, ground dry. 2 sections per battery move over HEBUTERNE - COLLINCAMPS Ridge to positions W of SERRE.	
	20th		Lieut. A.E. BIRTWISTLE 'C' from Army Artillery School.	
			Remainder of Batteries joined advanced sections. No registration or firing of any sort was done from these positions. Bde. H.Q. moved to COLLINCAMPS.	
			2/Lieut. J.A. SHERRY attd 'A' from 42nd D.T.Ms.	
	21st	4.55 am.	Creeping barrage (from unregistered positions) put down by 211th Bde. for capture of Hill 140 W of MIRAUMONT. 125 and 127th Bdes. attacked and carried the hill. Owing to shortage of artillery the 210th and 211th Bdes. concentrated in barrage to take 125th Bde. over the hill 140 and BEAUREGARD DOVECOTE and repeated the barrage later to 127th Bde. over the lower southern slopes. New Zealand Div. attacked PUISIEUX on left flank, 21st Div. attacked BEAUCOURT on the right. 'B' and 'C' Btys. advanced two positions W of PUISIEUX.	
	22nd		Weather fine and ground dry. Barrage put down for recapture of BEAUREGARD DOVECOTE. Lieut.Colonel F.G. CROMPTON 'H.Q.' (posted from 62nd D.A.) assumes command of 211th Bde. vice Lt. Col. F.H. HUGHES DSO retained in U.K.	

Army Form C. 2118.

WAR DIARY
or
INTELLIGENCE SUMMARY.
(Erase heading not required.)

Instructions regarding War Diaries and Intelligence Summaries are contained in F. S. Regs., Part II. and the Staff Manual respectively. Title pages will be prepared in manuscript.

Place	Date 1918 Aug	Hour	Summary of Events and Information	Remarks and references to Appendices
Field	23rd		Weather fine, ground dry. In conjunction with attack on IRLES by N.Z. Div., 211th Bde. fired barrage to support 125 Bde. in clearing the valley N of MIRAUMONT. 'A' and 'B' Btys. occupy positions S of PUISIEUX. Lieut. E.M. FRY 'D' killed in action.	
	24th		MIRAUMONT captured. 'C' Bty crosses the ANCRE and comes into action W of PYS. Bde. H-Q. join 'D' S of PUISIEUX.	
	25th		211th Bde. passed under command of 63rd Div. 2 teams of 'C' Bty blown up by road mines. 211th Bde. move into position of readiness E of MIRAUMONT. Orders received from 6.R.A. 63rd Div. noon to come into action N of LOUPART WOOD. N.Z. Div. still on left, 21st Div. on right. S.O.S. call 63rd Div. answered in the evening. Weather fine, ground dry. Capt. G.A.S. COLLIN 'C' proceeded to U.K. on 14 days' leave.	
	26th		63 rd Div. made an unsuccessful attack on THILLOY under barrage by 210th, 211th, 123rd, and 223rd Bdes.	
	27th		211th Bde. Pass under orders of C.R.A. 42nd Div. 42nd Div. relieve 63 rd. Div. 2/Lieut. V.R. CLARKE 'B' admitted to hospital sick.	
	28th		Annihilating fire put down by 211th Bde. across S end of BAPAUME. 2/Lieut. H. TOPPING 'D' from leave in U.K. Major J. NALL attd. 'H.Q' rejoins 'A' Capt. R.W. GARDINER H-Q. attd. 'C'	
	29th		211th Bde. move to positions N of LE BARQUE - THILLOY having been evacuated by the enemy.	
	30th		Weather fine, ground dry. LE BARQUE and Wagons lines W of ALBERT - BAPAUME road shelled by 8". No casualties.	
	31st		Weather fine, ground dry.	

SUMMARY.

CASUALTIES	O.	ORs.			POSTINGS	O.	ORs.
Killed	1	4		From Hospital		-	70
Wounded	1	17		To Courses		2	11
To Hospital	2	48		From Courses		1	8
				From leave		6	59
				To Bde.		-	74
				From Bde.		-	48
				To Leave		4	122

211th. Brigade R.F.A.

WAR DIARY

SEPTEMBER 1918.

Volume No. 20

Army Form C. 2118.

WAR DIARY
or
INTELLIGENCE SUMMARY.
(Erase heading not required.)

Instructions regarding War Diaries and Intelligence Summaries are contained in F. S. Regs., Part II. and the Staff Manual respectively. Title pages will be prepared in manuscript.

Place	Date	Hour	Summary of Events and Information	Remarks and references to Appendices
In the Field	1st Sept 1918		Batteries come into action W. of REINCOURT. - Weather fine, ground dry. Capt. C.R.Brown A.211 Posted to & 5th. Div. Arty. Capt. C.I.Scowcroft A.211 Posted from 210th. Bde. R.F.A. Capt. R.W. Gardiner H.Q. Posted to C.211. Lieut. F.T.Blennerhassett C.211 posted to H.Q.	MC
	2nd.		Brigade fires barrage for capture of VILLERS AU FLOS. Weather fine, Heavy enemy bombing of Battery areas and BAPAUME Roads during night 1st/2nd. Water supply allows horses to be watered twice per day only. Section of C.211 attached to Battalion in line, relieved by one section A.211 2/lieut. P.W. Stevens A.211 Rejoins from leave in U.K.	MC
	3rd.		Weather fine. Section A.211 withdrawn to the Battery. Brigade advances to positions E. of VILLERS AU FLOS. 9 p.m. Brigade again advances to positions E. of BARASTRE. Occasional fire maintained on NEUVILLE BOURJONVAL. Heavy enemy bombing during night 3/4th.	MC
	4th.		Brigade comes into action W. of BUS and fires creeping barrage immediately on arrival for capture of NEUVILLE. Considerable amount of enemy gas in forward areas. Weather fine.	MC
	5th.		Brigade advances into action W. of YTRES. Creeping barrage fired for capture of trenches E. of NEUVILLE. Brigade comes under orders of N.Z. Div. Arty. N.Z. Division relieves 42nd. Div. in centre Sector. 37th. Div. relieve N.Z. Div. in Left Sector. Corps front reduced to two Divisional fronts. V Corps on right. Weather fine.	MC
	6th.		Major J.Nall A.211 To U.K.on 14 days leave.	MC
	7th.		211th. Bde. withdrawn from action.	MC
	8th.		Brigade marches to BEAULENCOURT Brigade at rest. Rain all day. Orders received at 5 p.m. to return to action on 9th. inst. 2/Lieut. J.W.Tindell A.211 Posted to C.211. Lieut. G. Stephenson C.211 Posted to B.211.	MC
	9th.		Rain all morning. Brigade marches to YTRES and comes under orders of N.Z.D.A.	MC
	10th.		Ammunition taken to positions selected S. of METZ. Rain all day. All guns taken into action S. of METZ at YTRES. Enemy night bombing. Guard mounted on guns. Personnel remain in wagon lines Capt. G.A.S. Collin C.211 Rejoins from leave in U.K. and posted to 5th. Div. Arty.	MC
	11th.		Rain all day. Personnel moved up to the guns leave. Capt. F. Knowles B.211 To U.K. on 14 days leave.	MC
	12th.		Creeping barrage fired in support of N.Z. Div. attack on high ground W. of GOUZEAUCOURT in conjunction with general IV and VI Corps attacks. VI Corps on left of IV. 37th. Div. on Left Sector. IV Corps N.Z. Div. in Right Sector. 38th. Div., V Corps on right of N.Z.Div. Standing barrage fired during late afternoon for consolidation of final objective. Fine noon rain all evening and night. Lieut. J.Almond B.211 Attached to R.A.H.Q.	MC

Army Form C. 2118.

WAR DIARY
or
INTELLIGENCE SUMMARY.
(Erase heading not required.)

Instructions regarding War Diaries and Intelligence Summaries are contained in F. S. Regs., Part II. and the Staff Manual respectively. Title pages will be prepared in manuscript.

Place	Date	Hour	Summary of Events and Information	Remarks and references to Appendices
In the Field	Sep 1918 13th. 14th.		The Brigade withdraws to wagon line area E. of YTRES. Weather fine. Resting. Cloudy but fine. 10 p.m. orders received for three days rest time to be spent in games, sleep, grazing and bathing. 4.30 a.m. night 14/15th. orders received to stand to in readiness to move at 5.30 a.m. to rear positions to cover CORPS line in case of enemy attack. No attack, resting continued at 7 a.m. Orders for reconnaissance of rear positions near BUS received and carried out.	W/C W/C
	15th.		Thunderstorm night 15/16th. Heavy enemy bombing of YTRES area. 85 Horses and Mules B. & C Bty. killed, 38 evacuated, 75 wounded. 2/Lieut. J.A.Croll D.211 to 3rd. Army Arty. Course. Lieut. H.E.Beard A.211 Rejoins from 3rd. Army Arty. Course.	W
	16th.	5.30 p.m.	A. & C btys. reconnoitred for positions N. of HAVRINCOURT WOOD - Bde. buries horses. Brigade moves camp to area round BERTINCOURT. Showers - dull. Night 16/17th. heavy thunderstorm, all tents and bivouacs of A. & C Btys. blown away. Lieut. H.W.L.Kearns A.211 posted to 42nd. R.A.H.Q.	W W/C
	17th.		Weather changeable - Rest continues. Orders received for Brigade to rest up to midnight 19/20th. Lieut. A.E. Birtwistle C.211 To U.K on 14 days leave.	W/C
	18th.	11 a.m. 7 p.m.	Orders received for Bde. to be in readiness to move to area 1st Army at short notice. Orders received for Bde. and Battery Commanders to report at once at 37th. Div. H.Q. VELU. Rear positions W. of VELU to cover CORPS line reconnoitred by all B.Gs and for Bde. to stand to.	W
	19th.		Bde. remains bivouaced but ready to move at short notice. Orders received at 5 p.m for Bde. to be put in readiness to move night 19/20th. to BULLECOURT, orders cancelled 8.50 p.m. Period of rest expires midnight 19th/20th. Weather fine. Rest continues. 2/Lieut. W.K.Carter B.211 Posted from D.A.C.	W
	20th. 21st to 24th.		Training under Section Commanders. Training continued Weather fine. 23rd. Capt. M.F. Thompson D.211 to U.K On 14 days leave.	W W
	25th.		Night of 25/26th. guns of all four Batteries taken into position N.E. corner of HAVRINCOURT WOOD. Guard mounted on guns.	W
	26th.		Night 26th. personnel of Brigade occupies the gun position. Weather fine.	W

Army Form C. 2118.

WAR DIARY
or
INTELLIGENCE SUMMARY.
(Erase heading not required.)

Instructions regarding War Diaries and Intelligence Summaries are contained in F.S. Regs., Part II. and the Staff Manual respectively. Title pages will be prepared in manuscript.

Place	Date	Hour	Summary of Events and Information	Remarks and references to Appendices
In the Field	27th Sept 1918	5.20 a.m.	Creeping barrage fired covering 125th. INF. Bde. In attack by 3rd. Army on HINDENBURG line S. of FLESQUIERES RRI RIDGE. Rain early morning 27th. but fine all day. 1 F.O.O supplied by the Brigade. 5th. Division on right. 3rd. division on left. Left successful, right held up. Capt. F. Knowles B.211 Rejoins from leace in U.K.	W.C.
	28th	2.15 a.m.	Creeping barrage fired to cover 125 INF. Bde. for continuation of attack on HIGHLAND RIDGE. During afternoon Bde. advance into action S. of RIBECOURT and passed under Command of C.R.A. N.Z. Div.	W.C.
	29th		Creeping barrage fired 5.30 a.m. to cover N.Z. Inf. for attack on LA VACQUIEREE and BONAVIS RIDGE Weather fine. Lieut. H.E. Beard A.211 To U.K on 14 days leave.	W.C.
	30th		The Brigade came into position of readiness 6 a.m. in COUILLET VALLEY. Cloudy, strong wind. 1 p.m. The Brigade moved into action N.E. of LA VACQUERIE. Considerable delay. Difficulty in occupying these positions as the Brigade was the first to cross HINDENBURG System on WELSH RIDGE. Water supply very limited afterleaving HAVRINCOURT. Major J. Nail A.211 Granted extension leave Medical Certificate War Office.	W.C.

SUMMARY.

	O.	O.R.		O.	O.R.
Casualties.			Postings		
Killed	-	1	To Bde.	2	86
Wounded	1	24	From Bde.	2	19
To Hospital	-	65	From leave	2	113
From "	-	19	To "	5	105
To Courses	1	11			
From "	1	18			

Vol 21

Confidential

211th. Brigade R.F.A.

WAR DIARY
OCTOBER 1918.

Volume No, 21.

WAR DIARY
or
INTELLIGENCE SUMMARY.
(Erase heading not required.)

Army Form C. 2118.

Oct. 1918

Place	Date	Hour	Summary of Events and Information	Remarks and references to Appendices
Field.	1		Weather fine. Batteries remained in their positions doing harassing fire	
	2-4		Lieut. A.B. Dyke B.211 to Third Army Rest Camp.	
	2		Lieut. A.E. Birtwistle C.211 rejoins from leave in U.K.	
	3		Bde. moved forward to valley S. of Crevecoeur to support attack by N.Z. Div. on LESDAIN and ESNES.	
	4		which took place on 6th, and was completely successful. 2/Lieut. J.P. Heyworth B.211 posted from D.A.C.	
	5.		Major D. Brown B.211 to U.K. on 14 days' leave.	
			Major J. Nall A.211 rejoins from leave in U.K.	
	6.		Bde. cross the Canal D'ESCAUT and took up positions W of LESDAIN. Orders received at 20.00 hrs to move at once to take up positions about 1000 yds. S.E. of LESDAIN ready to fire on barrage following morning to support N.Z. in attack on BEAUVOIS 7th. 2/Lieut. J.A. Lechertier A.211 posted to D.211. Lieut. D. Malcolm A.211 posted from R.A.H.Q.	
	8.		Remained at ESNES.	
	9.		Bde. at rest.	
	10.		Capt. C.I. Scowcroft A.211 posted to D.A.C. Capt. M.F. Thompson D.211 rejoined from leave in UK	
	11.	1300	Bde. ordered to take up positions ready to support an attack by 42nd Div. to effect crossing of River SELLE. Positions selected 1000 yds. N.W. of VEISLY. Bde. settled in position about 2100 hrs. Lieut. A.C. Sandys D.211 to U.K. on 14 days' leave.	
	12	1400	Zero hour. Attack successful.	
			Major J. Nall A.211 G.S.W. Captain L.D. Mack HQ.211 G.S.W. Lieut. F.T. Blennerhassett HQ.211 G.S.W. 2/Lieut. H. Topping D.211 attd. H.Q.211. Capt. R. Hartley D.211 posted from R.A.H.Q. 210 Bde AFA	
	13-18		Still in action at VEISLY	
	14		2/Lieut. J.A. Croll D.211 rejoins from Artillery School. Lieut. J.A. Sherry attd. D.211 from 42nd T.Ms.	
	15.		2/Lieut. T. Knowles D.211 proceeded to U.K. on 14 days' leave.	
	16.		Lieut. F.T. Blennerhassett HQ.211 rejoins from hospital and appointed Adjutant with effect from 14.10.18. 2/Lieut. H. Topping attd. H.Q.211 to B.211.	
	19.		Bde. move to positions 1500 yds. E. ready to support attack the following morning. Lieut. G.H. Stephenson B.211 to U.K. on 14 days' leave. Lt.Colonel F.G. Crompton HQ.211 to Hospital sick. Lieut. A.B. Dyke B.211 rejoins from Rest Camp. Major V. Kilvert C.211 attd. H.Q.211.	
	20.	0200	42nd Div. - 126 and 127 bdes. attacked with 62nd Div. on Rt. and 5th Div. on Left. Objectives of 42nd Div. sunken roads on high ground running N. and S. about 1200 yds. W of VERTIGNEUL.	

Army Form C. 2118.

WAR DIARY
or
INTELLIGENCE SUMMARY.
(Erase heading not required.)

OCT 1918

Place	Date	Hour	Summary of Events and Information	Remarks and references to Appendices
	21st		attack completely successful. Barrage called off before final protective line reached. 2/Lieut. W.H. Shelly B.211 G.S.W. 2/Lieut. J.W. Tindell C.211 to hospital gas effects. Bde. crossed R.SELLE - C.211 leading. and took up positions E. of Road and W. of Railway About 1500 yards S. of SOLESMES.	
	22nd.		Lieut. G.H. Drewry H.Q. Posted from RAHQ. Lieut G. Stephenson B.211 To U.K on 14 days leave.	
	23rd.		Preparation for continuation of attack on 23rd. Inst. 42nd. Div., 125 Bde. attacks with 3rd. Division on left and 5th. Div. on right. Zero hour 2 a.m. - Barrage commenced at Zero plus 80 - Objective of 42nd. High Ground from ROMERIES to VENDEGIES au BOIS. This was successful after which the New Zealand Divn. assumed the advance capturing the village of NEUVILLE and High Ground N. and S. Brigade as soon as Barrage was finished at once advanced into position 1000 yds. S.E. of VERTIGNEUL ready to support a renewal of the advance Zero plus 612. The whole of the Bde. was in position and lines laid out three quarters of an hour before time for barrage to commence. Objective Crossing of the River ST. GEORGES and the capture of BEAUDIGNIES which was effected to time. Capt. M.F. Thompson D.211 posted as A/Major to A.211. Major D. Brown B.211 Rejoins from leave in U.K. Lieut A.B. Dyke B.211 To U.K on 14 days leave	
	24th.		Brigade moved at 5 am. into position of readiness at about 1000 yds E. of PONT A PIERRE advancing at 9 am. to positions 2000 yds W.S.W. of BEAUDIGNIES. Major V. Kilvert C.211 ceases to be attached to H.Q. Major D. Brown B.211 att. H.Q. 2/Lieut. J.W. Tindell C.211 Rejoins from Hospital. Capt. R. Hartley D.211 Posted to D.A.C. Captain C.I Seowcroft D.211 Posted from D.A.C. Remained in action at above position.	
	25th. to 26th.		Brigade moves back to rest at ROMERIES.	
	27th. 28th. & 29th.		Brigade resting - shelled each night.	
	31st.		Relieved 210th. Bde. In the line at positions 1000 yds. W. of BEAUDIGNIES - Weather FAIR. Major A.F.J. Forsyth D.211 To U.K. on 14 days leave.	

SUMMARY.

	O.	OR.		O.	OR.
Casualties.					
Killed	-	8	From Hospital	1	18
Wounded	6	52	To Courses	-	2
To Hospital	1	93	From "	1	7
			From leave	5	92
			Postings		
			to Bde.	3	51
			from Bde.	1	3
			To Leave	5	94

Confidential

211th. Brigade R.F.A.

WAR DIARY
NOVEMBER 1918.

Volume No. 22.

Army Form C. 2118.

WAR DIARY
or
INTELLIGENCE SUMMARY.
(Erase heading not required.)

Nov 1918

Instructions regarding War Diaries and Intelligence Summaries are contained in F. S. Regs., Part II. and the Staff Manual respectively. Title pages will be prepared in manuscript.

Place	Date	Hour	Summary of Events and Information	Remarks and references to Appendices
In the Field	1st.		Harassing fire carried out and new positions reconnoitred for forthcoming operations. Weather fair. 2/Lieut. J.W. Tindell C.211 To U.K on 14 days leave.	
	2nd.		One Section of each Battery moved into new positions. Harassing fire carried out on enemy roads and posts. Capt. A.E.Birtwistle A.210 attached to C.211. Major V.Kilvert C.211 admitted to Hospital - N.Y.D.	
	3rd.		Remainder of Batteries move to new positions. Location E. edge of Beaudignies- weather wet. 2/Lieut. T. Knowles D.211 Rejoins from leave in U.K. 2/Lieut R.J.Hatfield C.211 Posted from R.A.H.Q.	
	4th.		Zero hour 5.30 am N.Z. Div. attacks with 37th Div. on right and 62nd. Div on left. Objective of N.Z. Div.- capture of LE QUESNOY and ground up to a line running approx. N. and S. through villages of POTELLE and VILLEREAU, after which the Bde. with the exception of D.211 (Who had suffered heavy casualties having also had 5 Hows put out of action) moved forward to positions 1500 yds. S. of LE QUESNOY to carry forward barrage to final objective. N.Z. line running N. and S. through HERBIGNIES which was effected to time. After which Bde. remained Div Reserve Infantry advancing beyond this line. Garrison of LE QUESNOY surrounded since 10.00 hours surrendered late in the afternoon. 2/Lieut. J.A. Lechertier D.211 Killed in action.	
	5th.		Batteries remained in their present positions. Lieut E.A. Marr 42nd. T.Ms attached to B.211. Lieut. C.V. Wilcox 42nd. T.Ms attached to A.211. Capt. J.Myerscough (R.C. Chaplain) to U.K on 14 days leave.	
	8th.		Lieut. G.H Stephenson B.211 rejoins from leave in U.K.	
	9th.		Brigade move forward into positions 800 yds E. of HAUTMONT. Enemy reported retiring and Infantry out of touch.	
	10th.		Brigade remained in position.	
	11th.		Wire received stating Armistice had been arranged and hostilities would cease at 11.00 hours.	
	12th.		Lieut. A.B.Dyke B.211 rejoins from leave in U.K.	
	13th.		Bde. H.Q. only moves to Chateau BOUSSIERES. Lieut H.E. Beard A.211 Posted to C.211 on rejoining from leave in U.K.	
	14th.		Representatives from Bde. attended Commemoration Service at HAUTMONT Church in memory of prisoners and others who died whilst HAUTMONT was in German hands. Capt. R.W. Gardiner C.211. rejoins from leave in U.K.	

WAR DIARY
or
INTELLIGENCE SUMMARY.

(Erase heading not required.)

Army Form C. 2118.

Place	Date	Hour	Summary of Events and Information	Remarks and references to Appendices
In the Field.	Nov 1918 16th.		Captured 4.2 and 77 mm guns presented to Maire and Townspeople of HAUTMONT - Gun teams provided by C and D.211. H.Q. and each Battery also were represented by dismounted party. Capt. A.E.Birtwistle attached C.211 Rejoins /.210 Bde R.F.A.	
	24th.		Capt. F.T.Blennerhassett H.Q. to U.K on 14 days leave.	
	25th.		2/Lieut. V.R. Clarke B.211 Posted from Base.	
	26th.		Lieut. Colonel F.G.Crompton H.C. Rejoins from sick leave. Major D Brown att H.Q. rejoins B.211.	

SUMMARY

	O.	O.R.	Postings	O.	O.R.
Casualties					
Killed	1	11	To Bde.	2	229
Wounded	1	16	From Bde.	2	70
To Hospital	1	162	Fromleave	9	179
From Hospital	1	80	To Leave	5	52
To Courses		5	From Courses		4

WR 23

211th. Brigade R.F.A.

WAR DIARY.
DECEMBER 1918.
Volume No 23.

Army Form C. 2118.

WAR DIARY
or
INTELLIGENCE SUMMARY.
(Erase heading not required.)

Instructions regarding War Diaries and Intelligence Summaries are contained in F.S. Regs. Part II. and the Staff Manual respectively. Title pages will be prepared in manuscript.

Place	Date	Hour	Summary of Events and Information	Remarks and references to Appendices
In the Field	Dec 1918			
	1st. to 13th.		General Training of Brigade, Gun Drill, Laying, Musketry, Saluting and Marching Drill, Route Marches, Recreation etc.	
	3rd.		2/Lieut. H. Nixon att. D.211 from 42nd. Div. T.Ms.	
	4th.		V.R. Clarke B.211 To Hospital - Influenza.	
	6th.		Lieut. E.A. Marr att. D.211 (from T.Ms) Att to 42nd. D.A.G.	
	8th.		2/Lieut. A.J. Rogerson A.211 To U.K on 14 days leave.	
	9th.		J.A. Croll D.211 Rejoins from leave in U.K. 2/Lieut. A. Young C.211 To U.K. on 14 days leave.	
	11th.		Capt. Rev. J. Myerscough att H.Q. Posted to No 4 Stationary Hospital.	
	14th.		211th. Bde. commence trek by Route Marcj to MONTIGNIES-sur-SAMBRE near CHARLEROI. Brigade billeted for the night at JEUMONT.	
	15th.		Lieut. A.C. Sandys D.211 To Hospital - Pyrexia. Trek continued - Bde. billeted at THUIN on night of 15th.	
	16th.		Bde. rests at THUIN for 2 days.	
	17th.		Capt. F.T. Blennerhassett H.Q. Rejoins from leave in U.K General Inspection of men, horses and vehicles prior to last stage of trek.	
	18th.		Bde. moves to MONTIGNIES-sur-SAMBRE and billeted in that area.	
	19th.		Capt. R.P. Bloor att B.211 Rejoins 42nd. Div. T.Ms	
	20th. to 31st.		Educational Classes commences, general Training and Recreation.	
	21st.		Preliminary Demobilization of Bde. commences.	
	22nd.		2/Lieut. H. Topping D.211 Conducting Officer to U.K with Demobilization Party.	
	23rd.		Capt. F. Knowles B.211 Att to 42nd. R.A.H.Q.	
	24th.		Capt. R.P. Bloor att B.211 Rejoins 42nd. Div. T.Ms. 2/Lieut. J.P. Heyworth B.211 Conducting Officer to U.K with Demobilization Party.	
	26th.		2/Lieut. W.N. Gryer A.211 To U.K on 14 days leave. 2/Lieut. J.W. Tindell C.211 att to A.211.	
	27th.		Major M.F. Thompson A.211 To B.Us Course SHOEBURYNESS. Lieut A.C. Sandys D.211 From Hospl.	
	29th.		2/Lieut. P.W. Stevens A.211 To U.K for duty under Ministry of Labor. 2/Lieut. A. Young C.211 Rejoins from leave in UK.	
			H. Nixon att D.211 att to A.211.	

SUMMARY

Postings	Off.	O.Rs		Off.	ORs.
To Hospital	2	71	To Bde.	3	36
From Hospl.	1	42	From Bde.	3	31
To Courses	1	1	From leave	-	104
To U.K for duty under Ministry of Labour	1	-	To Leave		
From Courses	-	5	Demobilized		

211th. Brigade R.F.A.

WAR DIARY
JANUARY 1919.

Volume No.24.

WAR DIARY
or
INTELLIGENCE SUMMARY.

(Erase heading not required.)

Army Form C. 2118.

Jan 1919

Place	Date	Hour	Summary of Events and Information			Remarks and references to Appendices
Montignies-sur-Sambre.	1st.		Capt. L.D.MACK and Capt. G.A.S.COLLIN (late 211th. Bde.) Awarded M.C. (New Years Honors List).			WS
	6th.		Major D.BROWN B.211 Mentioned in Despatches.			WS
			2/Lieut. A.J.ROGERSON A.211 Rejoins from leave in U.K.			WS
	8th.		B.A.BLACKBOROW C.211 To U.K on 14 days leave.			WS
	9th.		" T. KNOWLES D.211 To No.4 Veterinary Hospital CALAIS.			WS
			Lieut. G.H.DREWRY H.Q. To U.K for Demobilization.			WS
	10th.		2/Lieut. J.A.SHERRY C.211 - do -			WS
	12th.		" W.K.CARTER B.211 To Hospital - Acc. Injury.			WS
			W.K.CARTER Rejoins from Hospital.			
	19th.		Lieut. G. STEPHENSON " To U.K for Demobilization.			
	20th.		Presentation of Medal Ribbons to R.A. by Divisional Commander.			
	21st.		2/Lieut. W.K.CARTER B.211 To U.K. on 14 days leave.			
	23rd.		Capt. F. KNOWLES att R.A.H.Q. Rejoins B.211.			
	26th.		Major C.R.BROWN att A.211 From 210th. Bde. R.F.A.			
			SUMMARY.			
				O.	O.Rs	
			To Hosp.	1	43	
			To Leave	2	63	
			Postings			
			To Bde.	1	21	
			From Bde.	-	11	
				O.	O.Rs.	
			From Hospital	2	9	
			From Leave	2	22	
			To Courses	1	1	
			Demobilized	6	131	
			To U.K as Demobilizers	-	4	

WAR DIARY
211th. Brigade R.F.A.
FEBRUARY 1919.
Volume No.25

Army Form C. 2118.

WAR DIARY
or
INTELLIGENCE SUMMARY.
(Erase heading not required.)

Instructions regarding War Diaries and Intelligence Summaries are contained in F. S. Regs., Part II. and the Staff Manual respectively. Title pages will be prepared in manuscript.

Feb. 1919

Place	Date	Hour	Summary of Events and Information	Remarks and references to Appendices
MONTIGNIES sur SAMBRE	2nd.		2/Lieut. C.V.WILCOX att. A.211 To U.K for Demobilization.	App.
	3rd.		" A.J.ROGERSON " D.211 Posted to A.211.	
	4th.		Capt. D. MALCOLM att. A.211 To Hospital Sick	App.
			2/Lieut. J.W.TINDELL A.211 - do -	
	6th.		" R.J.HATFIELD H.Q. To U.K. on 14 days leave.	App.
	7th.		" W.K.CARTER B.211 Rejoins from leave in U.K and posted to A.211.	App.
	8th.		Major H.PICKARD C.211 To Hospital - Sick.	
	9th.		" D.BROWN B.211 To U.K for Demobilization.	App.
	14th.		2/Lieut J.W.TINDELL A.211 Rejoins from Hospital	
	20th.		Captain G.A.WALLIS B.211 Posted from 5th. Div. Arty.	App.
	25th.		" F.KNOWLES " To U.K for Demobilization.	App.
	27th.		Lieut V.R.CLARKE " To U.K on 14 days leave.	App.

SUMMARY

	Officers	O.Rs.		Officers	O.Rs.
To Hospital	3	14	To Courses	-	1
From Hospital	1	29	From Courses	-	1
To leave	2	212	Postings to Bde.	1	-
From leave	1	44	From Bde.	1	1
			Demobilized	3	135

WAR DIARY.
211th Brigade R.F.A
March '19.

Volume No. 26.

WAR DIARY or INTELLIGENCE SUMMARY.

Army Form C. 2118.

Place	Date	Hour	Summary of Events and Information			Remarks and references to Appendices
Montignies sur Sambre.	7th		2/Lieut. J.W. Tindell	C.211	to Hospital.	W/
	13th		2/Lieut. T. Knowles	D.211	from 4th Vety. Hospital Calais.	W/
	14th		Lieut. T.W. Morris	A.211	posted from 42nd D.A.C.	W/
			Lieut. J.J. Cowleson	C.211	" " " "	W/
			Lieut. C.R. Rivett	B.211	" " " "	W/
			2/Lieut. O.L. Quinn	C.211	" " " "	W/
			Lieut. Adams	D.211	" " " "	W/
	15th		Lieut. H.E. Beard	A.211	" C.211.	W/
	16th		Lieut. V.R. Clarke	B.211	from leave in U.K., and posted to D.211.	W/
	19th		Lieut. A.B. Dyke	B.211	posted to A of O. also Lieut T.W. Morris	W/
			2/Lieut. O.L. Quinn	C.211	" " " " 2/Lt. W.K. Carter.	W/
	20th		2/Lieut. J.A. Croll	D.211	to U.K. for demobilisation.	W/
	22nd		2/Lieut. R.J. Hatfield	HQ.211	attached to H.Q.211.	W/
	23rd		Lieut. H.E. Beard	A.211	from leave in U.K.	W/
	24th		Lieut.Colonel F.G. Crompton	H.Q.211		W/
			2/Lieut. H. Nixon	C.211		W/
			Major M.F. Thompson A.211 struck off strength from 30.1.19) Authority IV Corps letter A 84/9/729.			

SUMMARY.

	O.	O.Rs.		O.	O.Rs.
To Hospital	1	17	From Courses.	1	1
From Hospital	-	5	Postings to Bde.	8	51
To leave	1	28	" from "	3	208
From leave	3	7	Demobilised	2	16